Oxford
International
Primary

1

Science
Student Book

Deborah Roberts
Terry Hudson

Alan Haigh
Geraldine Shaw

Language consultants:
John McMahon
Liz McMahon

OXFORD

OXFORD
UNIVERSITY PRESS

Great Clarendon Street, Oxford, OX2 6DP, United Kingdom

Oxford University Press is a department of the University of Oxford. It furthers the University's objective of excellence in research, scholarship, and education by publishing worldwide. Oxford is a registered trade mark of Oxford University Press in the UK and in certain other countries.

First published in 2014

British Library Cataloguing in Publication Data

Data available

ISBN 978-1-382006545

9 10 8

Paper used in the production of this book is a natural, recyclable product made from wood grown in sustainable forests. The manufacturing process conforms to the environmental regulations of the country of origin.

Printed in China by Golden Cup

Acknowledgements

The publisher and authors would like to thank the following for permission to use photographs and other copyright material:

Cover: Artwork by Blindsalida. **Photos: p6(tl):** Zentilia/Shutterstock; **p6(tr):** Sergey Peterman/Shutterstock; **p6(m):** Bibiphoto/Shutterstock; **p9(b), 37(l):** Kozak Dmytro/Shutterstock; **p9(b), 40(br):** Valzan/Shutterstock; **p11(b):** Maks Narodenko/Shutterstock; **p12–13:** Rawpixel.com/Shutterstock; **p13(tl):** Tony Stock/Shutterstock; **p13(tr):** Kuttelvaserova Stuchelova/Shutterstock; **p13(ml):** Dirk Ercken/Shutterstock; **p13(mr):** Eric Isselee/Shutterstock; **p14(ml):**KAMONRAT/Shutterstock; **p14(m):** Viorel Sima/Shutterstock; **p14(mr):** Jo Crebbin/Shutterstock; **p14(bl):**Hitdelight/Shutterstock; **p14(br):** Labrador Photo Video/Shutterstock; **p15(l):** Ivy Close Images/Alamy Stock Photo; **p15(r):** Randy Duchaine/Alamy Stock Photo; **p15(m):** Travis Rowan/Alamy Stock Photo; **p16(ml):** Dave Allen Photography/Shutterstock; **p16(m):** Korbut Ivetta/Shutterstock; **p16(mr):** Ananth-tp/Shutterstock; **p16(bl):**PRILL/Shutterstock; **p16(br):** Galina Savina/Shutterstock; **p17(tl):** Pics-xl/Shutterstock; **p17(tm):** Mauritius images GmbH/Alamy Stock Photo; **p17(tr):** Marc Henauer/Shutterstock; **p20(bl):** Ferderic B/Shutterstock; **p20(br):**Anton_Ivanov/Shutterstock; **p20(bm):** Markuso/Shutterstock; **p22:** Absolute-india/Shutterstock; **p24:**Michaeljung/Shutterstock; **p25(t):** XiXinXing/Shutterstock; **p26(t):** Dora Zett/Shutterstock; **p26(m):** Zurijeta/Shutterstock; **p28(tr):** Olga Popova/Shutterstock; **p28(mr):** Galayko Sergey/Shutterstock; **p28(ml):** Olha Afanasieva/Shutterstock; **p28(b):** Nattika/Shutterstock; **p29(b):** JIANG HONGYAN/Shutterstock; **p29(ml):** Dorling Kindersley/Getty Images; **p29(mr):**Mario7/Shutterstock; **p29(bl):** Eric Isselee/Shutterstock; **p29(br):** Alluvion Stock/Shutterstock; **p32-33:**Photographee.eu/Shutterstock; **p32(bl), 50:** Nokinka/Shutterstock; **p33(m), 50:** HomeStudio/Shutterstock; **p33(bl):**Nykonchuk Oleksii/Shutterstock; **p33(bm):** Richard Peterson/Shutterstock; **p33(br):** Kostakirov/Shutterstock; **p34(ml):**Coprid/Fotolia; **p34(m):** Stockbyte/OUP; **p34(m):** Johanna Goodyear/Shutterstock; **p34(mr):**Garberophotography/Shutterstock; **p34(bl):** Xiangdong Li/Fotolia; **p34(bm):** Nuwatphoto/Fotolia; **p34(br):**Lubava/Shutterstock; **p35(tr):** Olga Martynenko/Shutterstock; **p37(l):** Africa Studio/Shutterstock; **p37(m):**Dudaeva/Shutterstock; **p37(m):** MrHanson/Shutterstock; **p37(r):** Baloncici/Shutterstock; **p37(r):** Dmitry_T/Shutterstock; **p38:** Micheko Productions, Inh. Michele Vitucci/Alamy Stock Photo; **p40(t):** Natthawon Chaosakun/Shutterstock; **p40(ml):**Viktor Kunz/Shutterstock; **p40(ml):** Design56/Shutterstock; **p40(mr):** Thunchanok tonuang/123RF; **p40(mr):** Diez artwork/Shutterstock; **p40(bl):** MNI/Shutterstock; **p40(bm):** Africa Studio/Shutterstock; **p41(bl):** Karkas/Shutterstock; **p41(bm):** EugeniaSt/Shutterstock; **p41(bm):** Babimu/Fotolia; **p41(br):** Vladitto/Shutterstock; **p42(ml):**Claudiofichera/Shutterstock; **p42(bl):** Rdonar/Shutterstock; **p42(mr):** ILYA AKINSHIN/Fotolia; **p42(br):** Evgeny Karandaev/Shutterstock; **p43(mr):** MarcelClemens/Shutterstock; **p44(ml):** Professional photography/Shutterstock; **p44(m):** Tesgro Tessieri/Fotolia; **p44(bl):** Nexus 7/Shutterstock; **p44(m):** Elenathewise/Fotolia; **p44(br):** Babimu/Fotolia; **p44(mr):** Jorge Salcedo/Shutterstock; **p46(m):** Liza1979/Shutterstock; **p46(b):** Oneo/Shutterstock; **p47(tl):** Serg64/Shutterstock; **p47(t):** Drpnncpptak/Shutterstock; **p47(tr):** CK Ma/Shutterstock; **p47(ml):** Dimec/Shutterstock; **p47(bl):** Ilona Koeleman/Shutterstock; **p47(br):** Moolkum/Shutterstock; **p48(tl):** Bogdan ionescu/Shutterstock; **p48(tr):**Trabachar/Shutterstock; **p48(ml):** Xstockerx/Shutterstock; **p48(mr):** Schab/Shutterstock; **p48(br):** docter_k/Shutterstock; **p49(a):** Venusangel/Dreamstime; **p49(b):** Photodisc/Getty Images; **p49(c):** Dennis Kitchen Studio, Inc./Oxford University Press; **p49(d):** Dennis Kitchen Studio, Inc./Oxford University Press; **p49(e):** Stockbyte/Getty Images; **p49(f):** Vitaly Titov & Maria Sidelnikova/Shutterstock; **p49(g):** Ingram/Alamy Stock Photo; **p49(h):** Ingram/Alamy Stock Photo; **p49(i):**Stockbyte/Getty Images; **p49(b):** Donna Beeler/Shutterstock; **p50(ml):** Nokinka/Shutterstock; **p50(bl):**HomeStudio/Shutterstock; **p51(ml):** Dmitry_T/Shutterstock; **p51(ml):** Trabachar/Shutterstock; **p51(mr):** Professional photography/Shutterstock; **p51(mr):** Babimu/Fotolia; **p54(t):** istanbulphotos/Shutterstock; **p54(b), 66(bm):** Anna Stowe/Alamy Stock Photo; **p56(t):** Marty/Bigstock; **p56(b):** Sculpies/Shutterstock; **p58(tl), 66(bl):** ImagIN.gr photography/Shutterstock; **p59(b):** JongBeom Kim/TongRo Images/Alamy Stock Photo; **p63, 67(tl):** MM Studios/Oxford University Press; **p65(l):** Cosma/Shutterstock; **p65(r):** Oknoart/Shutterstock; **p66(br):** Pecold/Shutterstock; **p67(tl):**HomeStudio/Shutterstock; **p67(tr):** R-O-M-A/Shutterstock; **p67(tr):** Shaun Wilkinson/Alamy Stock Photo; **p68-69:** Golden Pixels LLC/Alamy Stock Photo; **p70(bl), 83(tl):** Scooperdigital/Shutterstock; **p70(bl), 83(tl):** BasPhoto/Shutterstock; **p71(tr), 83(tr):** Vltaly Ilyasov/Shutterstock; **p74(mr):** Damian Money/Shutterstock; **p75(mr):** Simon Burt/Alamy Stock Photo; **p78(tr):**Chbaum/Shutterstock; **p78(b):** Mark Wardle/Alamy Stock Photo; **p79(t):** Leonid Smirnov/Shutterstock; **p79(b):** Christian Mueller/Shutterstock; **p81(bl):** Littlekidmoment/Shutterstock; **p82(tl):** Eric Isselee/Shutterstock; **p82(tr):** Glowimages RM/Alamy Stock Photo; **p84-85:** Paul Maguire/123RF; **p84(bl):** Yarbeer/Shutterstock; **p85(bl):** Belozorova Elena/Shutterstock; **p87(tl):** Zaneta Baranowska/Shutterstock; **p87(tl):** Dionisvera/Fotolia; **p87(tr):** Stockbyte/Getty Images; **p87(tr):** AS Food studio/Shutterstock; **p93(t):** Ulrich Willmunder/Shutterstock; **p93(m):** Tetyana Dotsenko/Shutterstock; **p94, 99(tl):** Vadym Zaitsev/123RF; **p99(tm):** John Cartwright/Alamy Stock Photo.

Artwork by Six Red Marbles and Q2A Media Services Pvt. Ltd.

Every effort has been made to contact copyright holders of material reproduced in this book. Any omissions will be rectified in subsequent printings if notice is given to the publisher.

Contents

How to Use this Book

This Student Book for *Oxford International Primary Science* forms part of your science lessons for this year. Your teacher will introduce the ideas through whole-class activities, then you will explore them in more detail using this book, before all coming back together to discuss what you have learned. Find out more at: www.oxfordprimary.com/international-science

Structure of the book

This book is divided into five units plus an introduction called *Being a Good Scientist* and a picture Glossary:

Being a Good Scientist
Unit 1 Exploring Animals
Unit 2 What is it Made of?
Unit 3 Pushes and Pulls
Unit 4 Making Sounds
Unit 5 Plants and Seasons
Glossary

Each unit covers a different strand of science.

You will need a science notebook to write in and to record your investigation results and conclusions.

Being a good scientist

To be a good scientist you need to be curious and ask questions. This section will help you think about how to develop your scientific skills to work like a scientist.

What you will find in each unit

There are three types of lessons:

Wow introduces each unit's scientific ideas and key words. It tells you what you will learn in the unit and lets you discuss what you already know.

Focused lessons cover the scientific knowledge and skills you need to learn this year.

In **What have I learned?** you review your understanding and show your teacher what you have learned about the unit.

What you will find in the lessons

Although each lesson is unique, they have common features:

loud quiet sound voice The words on the Wow pages are included in the picture glossary at the back of the book. You can add your own notes for each word.

Key words breathe feed Gives you the key words for the lesson.

In this lesson you will name the parts of the body. Tells you what you will learn in the lesson.

Questions to help you talk to each other and share ideas about the science you are learning and the investigations you do.

Practical and research activities to investigate and report on science topics. Sometimes your teacher will ask you to use different equipment, which is available in school. They may also ask you to carry out a test in a different way, to make sure you are safe.

Stretch zone Challenges you to take your learning further.

Key idea Summarises what you have learned.

Additional features

Think back Reminds you what has been covered before.

Science fact Interesting and amazing science facts.

Highlights the skills needed to be a good scientist.

Important notes about how to stay safe.

Teacher's Guide

There is a Teacher's Guide to help your teacher to work out the resources needed and to offer alternative activities and approaches.

Workbook

At the bottom of each page in this book is a link to a Workbook, where you can record your work and get extra practice to do in your lesson or at home.

Being a Good Scientist

Science is the study of the world around us. To be a good scientist you need to be curious and ask questions. This section will help you think about how to develop your scientific skills to work like a scientist.

Scientists look carefully at the world to explain why things happen and to guess if things may happen.

Science is used to develop new technologies. It also helps us to know more about health and diseases. This means we can develop medicines and machines to keep people healthy.

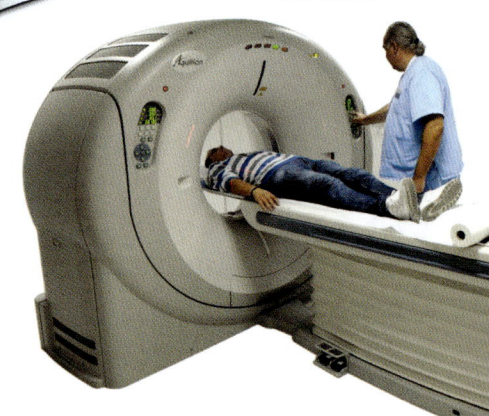

The diagram shows the steps you can take to find out about things (investigate) like a scientist.

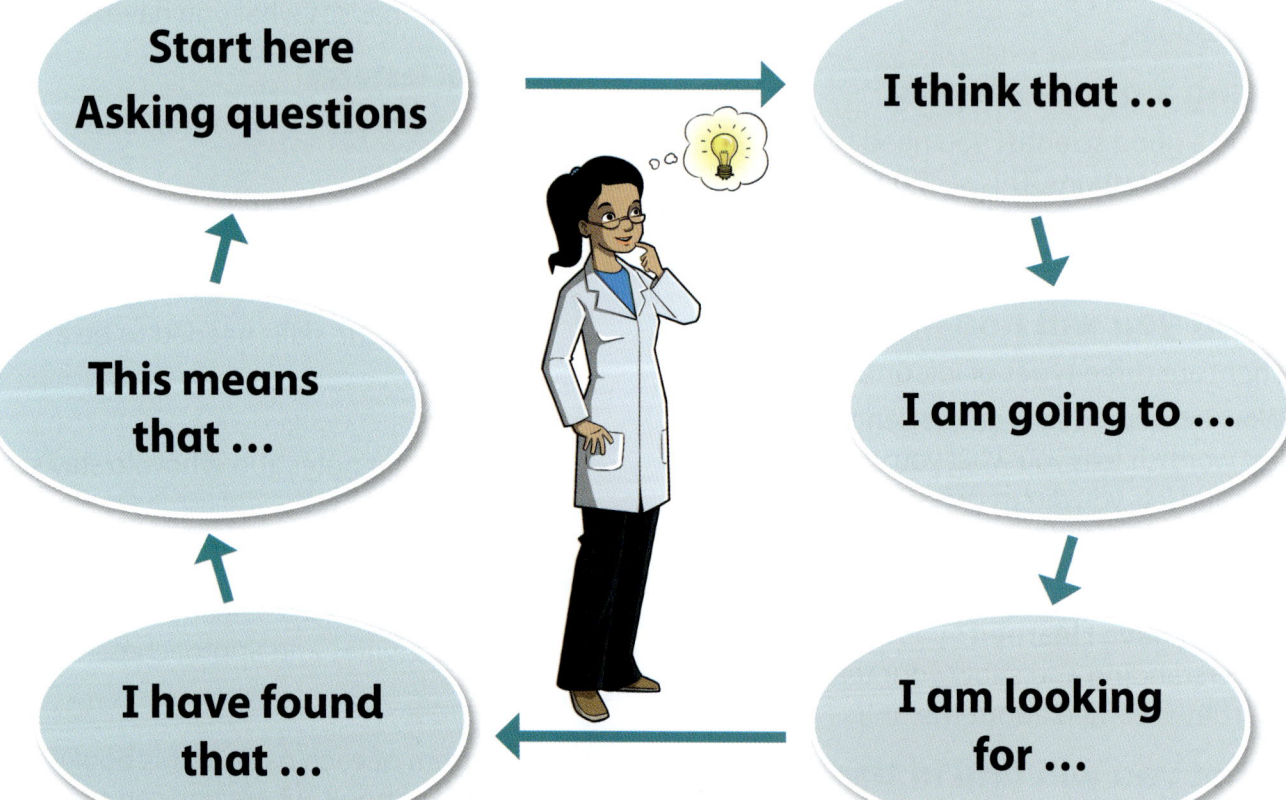

Start here
Asking questions

I think that ...

I am going to ...

I am looking for ...

I have found that ...

This means that ...

Learning to be a scientist allows you to develop scientific skills such as observing (looking), measuring and recording. It helps you to notice patterns in the things you observe and to sort things into groups. It also helps you to test our own ideas about how the world works.

Asking questions

Scientists ask questions about the world around them. This is called scientific enquiry.

A good way to start is to think of questions that start with words such as 'which', 'what', 'do' and 'does'.

Does all fruit taste sweet?

Which fruit do you like the most?

Think of your own questions to ask about your favourite fruit.

The questions you ask will give you a good start to your investigation.

I think that ...

Next, scientists try to work out or guess what will happen. Scientists call this a prediction.

They need to talk about their ideas and what they think will happen.

You might have already learned something about the question you are trying to answer. Scientists usually know something before they make predictions.

Use what you know about fruit to help you think about this question:

Which fruit tastes sweetest?

Do you think the orange or the grapes will taste sweetest?

What did you think about to help you choose?

I am going to ...

Scientists plan what they are going to do. They always discuss their plans before they start. This helps to check that the plan will work.

Scientists make their investigations fair by following some simple rules:

- They think about what they will keep the same.
- They think about what they will change.

For example, when investigating rainfall, you need to make sure no water is lost. This could happen from spills or water drying up in the Sun.

This makes sure that the only change is whether rain has fallen or not.

Scientists also think about the equipment they need. They make a list and make sure everything is available.

For example, if you are going to measure rainfall, you might make an equipment list like this:

Cup
Plastic bottle
Black marker pen
Ruler
Tape
Pebbles
Water in a jug

Science fact

Scientists do not always plan their own investigations. Sometimes they follow other scientist's plans. This is why it is very important to make the plans easy to follow.

Scientists look closely at what is happening in their investigation. They use all of their senses. These are called observation skills.

During an investigation you will look, listen, smell, touch and sometimes taste.

Warning! Only smell, taste and touch things if your teacher tells you it is safe. Many things can be poisonous.

You may need to use equipment to help with your observations. Some of the pieces of equipment you will use this year are shown below.

Good scientists use equipment carefully. They take a measurement more than once. This is to make sure they have not made any mistakes.

You can practise measuring the length of these lines. Which piece of equipment will you use? Tell your partner your measurements.

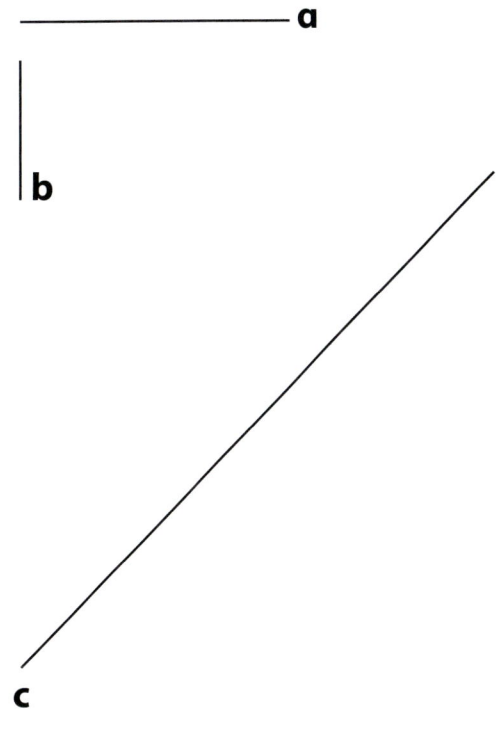

a

b

c

Scientists write down or record what they have found from their observations and measurements. This helps them to see patterns or to sort things into groups.

There are lots of different ways to record results.

Tables

One way is to complete a table.

You could use a table like this one to record the favourite fruits in your class:

Fruit	Number of students
orange	5
banana	4
apple	4
melon	6
kiwi	1

Look at the table. Answer these questions with your partner.

What is the least favourite fruit?

What is the most favourite fruit?

Ask the students in your class about their favourite colour.

Design a table for your results. Record the results in your table.

Charts

Results from tables can be shown as charts or graphs.

This chart shows the results of an investigation about colours.

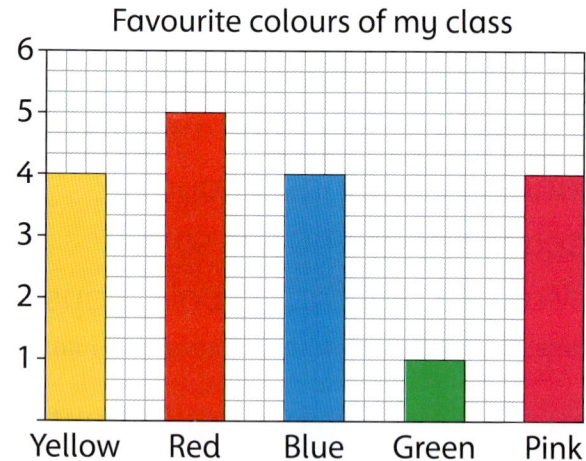

Favourite colours of my class

The number of students is plotted along the side on this chart.

The colour choices are plotted along the bottom.

What is the least favourite colour?

What is the most favourite colour?

Results are sometimes easier to read from charts than tables.

Drawings and models

Scientists may draw or make models of the things they are studying. Models help scientists to see and explain how things work. Science drawings are not like the pictures you paint. Scientific drawings are much simpler.

You might need to draw a plant or animal, or a piece of equipment.

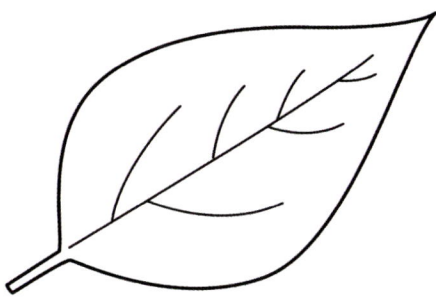

This is a simple drawing of a leaf but you can still tell what it is.

Photographs and videos

Scientists might also take photographs and video clips of their investigations and results.

This is a very accurate way to record results.

This means that ...

The last stage of an investigation is when scientists look at their results carefully.

They work out if the results have helped them to answer their investigation question.

The questions they might ask are:

Can I *see* any patterns?

Are any results unusual?

Was my prediction correct?

Could I have done anything *better*?

Finally, they will always think about how to make their investigation better.

It is useful to fill out an investigation planning form. This sets out all the stages of your investigation. It helps you to remember everything you need to think about. Your teacher can give you one of these.

1 Exploring Animals

In this unit you will:

- find out how we are all the same and all different

- discover and name some animals

- sort animals into groups

- name the parts of the body

- explore the senses of touch, taste, sight, hearing and smell.

Look at the photograph.

What is different about these children?

Say one thing that is the same about these children.

amphibian   bird
carnivore   fish
herbivore   mammal
omnivore   reptile
senses

How are these animals the same? How are they different?

Science fact

There are more than 7 billion people on Earth and they are all different. That is why each of us is special.

■ For more activities, go to Workbook 1 pages 12–13.

Sorting animals

In this lesson you will find out how we can sort living things into groups.

Key words
feature
group
skeleton
vertebrate/
invertebrate

Scientists have sorted animals into groups. This makes it easier to learn about them.

To do this, scientists study different features. They study what the animals look like. They also look at where the animals live, what they eat and how they move.

parrot

rabbit

eagle

camel

chicken

Work with your science partner to discuss these animals.

Can you sort them into two groups?

Is it possible to make equal groups? Why?

List the features you used to sort them.

■ For more activities, go to Workbook 1 page 14.

Some animals have a skeleton inside their body. Part of this is a backbone. Scientists call these animals vertebrates.

Other animals have shells, or no hard parts at all. Scientists call these animals invertebrates.

Look at the x-ray photographs.

Which show vertebrates? Which show invertebrates?

Talk with a partner about why you made these choices.

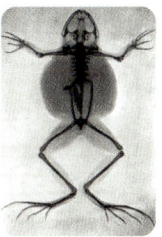
frog

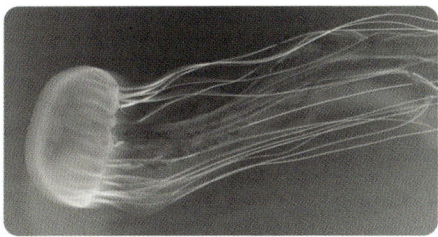
jelly fish

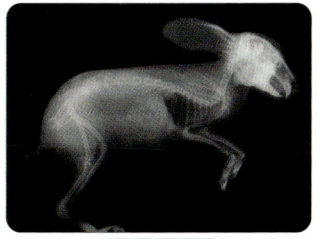
rabbit

Researching vertebrates and invertebrates

Your group will be given one of the animals in the word box to research:

1 Use books, magazines or the internet to find out about your animal.

2 Decide if it is a vertebrate or an invertebrate.

3 Find out where the animal lives and what it eats.

4 Draw the animal or cut out photographs you have found.

5 Your teacher will give you a paper plate to present your findings.

6 Walk around and look at the other plates.

camel
butterfly
worm
rabbit
spider
horse
bird
snail
crab
jelly fish

Stretch zone

How can snakes move without legs?

Key idea

We can put animals that are like each other into a group.

■ For more activities, go to Workbook 1 page 15.

The vertebrate groups

In this lesson you will sort vertebrate animals into smaller groups.

Key words
amphibian
bird
fish
mammal
reptile

Think back

How are vertebrates different from invertebrates?

Vertebrates can be split into five smaller groups called classes.

Science fact

Scientists identify large groups of animals by splitting them into smaller groups. Each group is called a class.

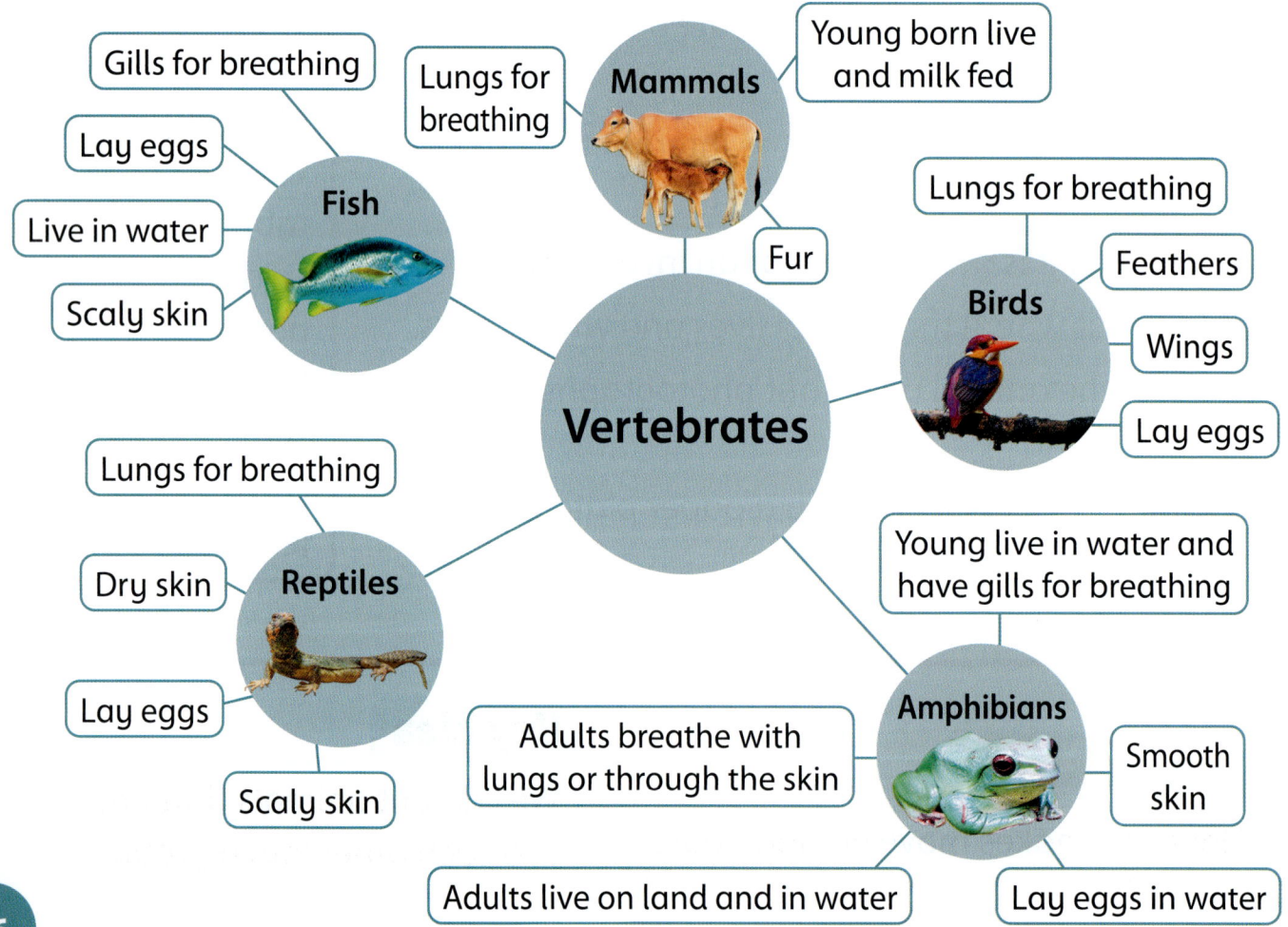

Gills for breathing

Lungs for breathing

Mammals

Young born live and milk fed

Lay eggs

Fish

Live in water

Fur

Lungs for breathing

Scaly skin

Feathers

Birds

Wings

Vertebrates

Lay eggs

Lungs for breathing

Dry skin

Reptiles

Young live in water and have gills for breathing

Lay eggs

Adults breathe with lungs or through the skin

Amphibians

Smooth skin

Scaly skin

Adults live on land and in water

Lay eggs in water

■ For more activities, go to Workbook 1 page 16.

Look at the photographs.
Decide which vertebrate class each animal belongs to.
List the features you used to help you decide.

1

2

3

Vertebrate survey

You are going to look for different vertebrates.

1 Write a list of those you see.

2 Write down your results in a table. Here is an example.

Vertebrates seen	How many did you see?
Amphibians	
Birds	
Fish	
Mammals	
Reptiles	

3 Tell your class about your results.

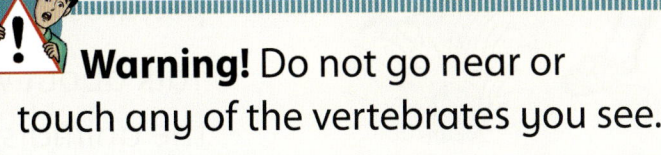

Warning! Do not go near or touch any of the vertebrates you see.

Stretch zone

Whales live and feed in the ocean.
Guess which vertebrate class whales belong to.
Use the internet or books to check your guess.

Key idea

We can sort vertebrates into five smaller groups.

■ For more activities, go to Workbook 1 page 17.

What eats what?

In this lesson you will explore animals that are carnivores, herbivores and omnivores.

Key words
carnivore
herbivore
omnivore
pet

Think back

How many different vertebrates did you find in your area? What do they eat?

Animals and humans have to eat to stay alive. The food they eat gives them energy. It helps them to grow.

Animals that eat plants are called herbivores.

Animals that eat other animals are called carnivores.

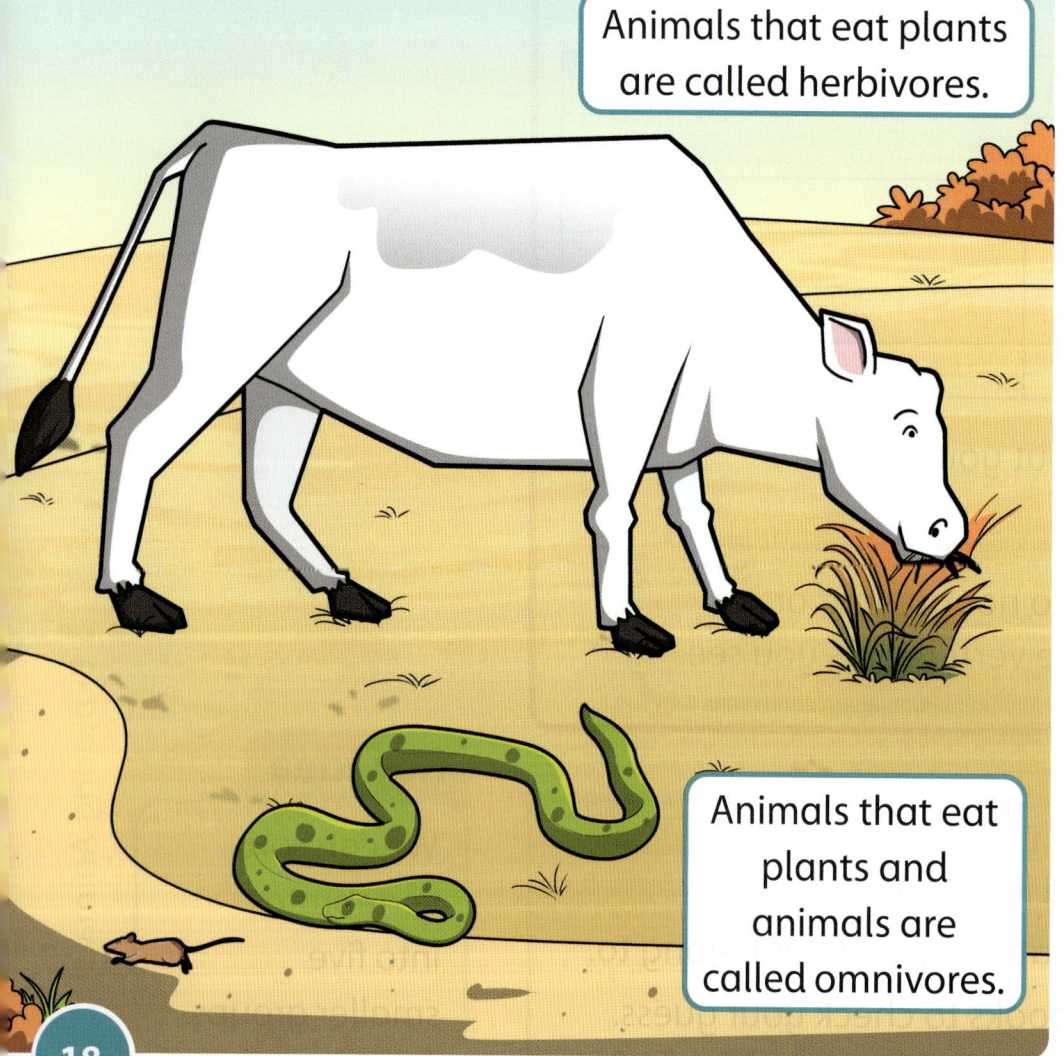

Animals that eat plants and animals are called omnivores.

Look at the pictures.

Talk about what the animals and the person are doing.

What would happen to the cow if it did not eat the grass?

■ For more activities, go to Workbook 1 page 18.

Pet survey

1 Ask the people in your class if they have a pet.

2 Ask them what their pet eats.

3 Decide if the pet is a carnivore, a herbivore or an omnivore.

4 Write a table like the one below in your notebook.

Type of pet	What it eats	Herbivore, carnivore or omnivore?

5 Draw a poster about three different pets. Choose one carnivore, one herbivore and one omnivore.

6 Show what they eat and how they are looked after.

Look at the pictures on page 18.

Which are herbivores?

Which are carnivores?

Is there an omnivore?

Key idea

Animals can be sorted into herbivores, carnivores and omnivores by what they eat.

Stretch zone

Write a list of the food you have eaten this week.

Are you a carnivore, a herbivore or an omnivore? Explain why.

1 Exploring Animals

19

■ For more activities, go to Workbook 1 page 19.

Sorting some unusual animals

In this lesson you will learn about some animals that are not easy to sort into groups.

Key words
breathe
feed

Some animals look as if they belong to one group. But look closely and you will have to think again!

Think back

Talk to your partner about the features you used to group vertebrates.

Look at each photograph.

Decide which vertebrate class each animal belongs to.

Why are the animals unusual?

I live in the sea.
I must come to the surface to breathe. I feed my offspring on milk. Which group do I belong to?

I live in the sea for half my life. I must come to the surface to breathe. I have feathers. Which group do I belong to?

I have wings. I can fly. I have fur. Which group do I belong to?

■ For more activities, go to Workbook 1 page 20.

Bird feeders

You are going to set up bird feeders to attract different types of birds.

1 Make feeders like the ones in the pictures.
2 Look at your feeders every morning and afternoon. Do this for 3 days.
3 Write down how many different types of bird visit your feeders. Take photographs if you can.
4 Try to sort the birds into smaller groups.
5 Were any of the birds unusual and difficult to group?

Stretch zone

Find out the features that scientists use to divide the class of birds into smaller groups.

Be a scientist

Scientists make observations at different times of the day and over many days.

▶ page 9

Key idea

Some animals with unusual features are more difficult to sort.

■ For more activities, go to Workbook 1 page 21.

Same but different

In this lesson you will find out how we are all the same and all different.

Which parts of the body can you name? Compare what you know with your partner.

We usually have a nose, two eyes, two ears, a mouth and hair. But each face is different.

We can compare our faces with other people's faces.

Key words
ears
eyes
face
head
hair
mouth
nose

Comparing your face to others

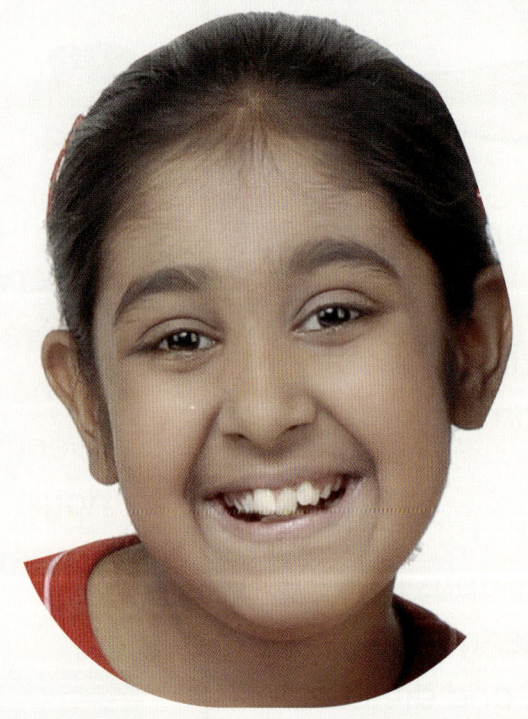

1 Point to a part of the face in the photograph and say out loud what it is called.

2 Your teacher will give you a mirror. Look in the mirror and point to the same part on your face.

How is your face different from everyone else's face?

22

■ For more activities, go to Workbook 1 page 22.

Drawing faces

1 Draw your face in your notebook. Use this diagram to help you label it.

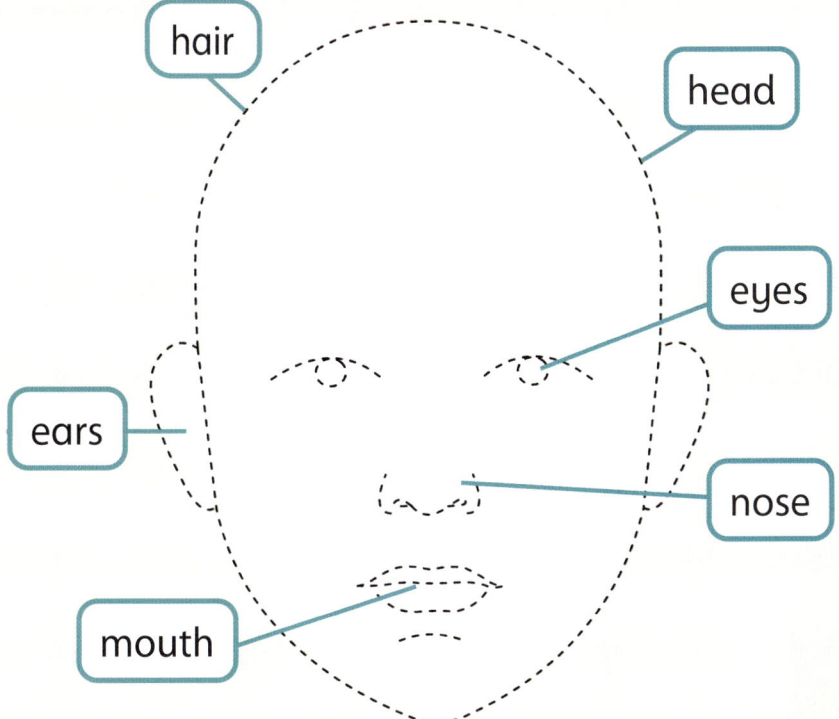

hair

head

eyes

ears

nose

mouth

2 Practise making a happy face and a sad face using a mirror.

3 Draw your happy and sad faces in your notebook.

What is the difference between the happy and the sad face?

Stretch zone

Can you show someone you are happy or sad if they can only see your eyes? Explain why.

Key idea

We are not all the same but we do usually have some of the same features: a nose, two eyes, two ears and a mouth.

■ For more activities, go to Workbook 1 page 23.

Our body

In this lesson you will name the parts of the body.

Key words

arms
body
head
legs

Naming parts of the body

1 Read the words in the box. Find these parts of the body on the photograph.

head	neck	face	teeth	elbow
arm	hand	leg	knee	foot

2 Point to three of these on your own body.

Stretch zone

Can you point to your fingers, toes and shoulders?

Talk to your partner about how you are different from the person in the photograph. Look at each of the body parts.

24

■ For more activities, go to Workbook 1 page 24.

Talk about the people in the photograph. Look at their arms, legs and heads.

How are the people different?

How are they the same?

Sing the song 'Head, shoulders, knees and toes'. Point to each part of the body as you sing them.

Key idea

We have names for the parts of our body.

■ For more activities, go to Workbook 1 page 25.

Our senses: seeing, hearing

In this lesson you will learn about our senses.

Key words
animal
hear/hearing
human
senses
sight/seeing

Humans (people) and animals have five senses: seeing, hearing, tasting, smelling and touching.

Our senses help us to find out about the world.

Talk about the photograph of the cat.

Which part of the cat lets it **hear** things?

Which part of the cat helps it **see** things?

Seeing

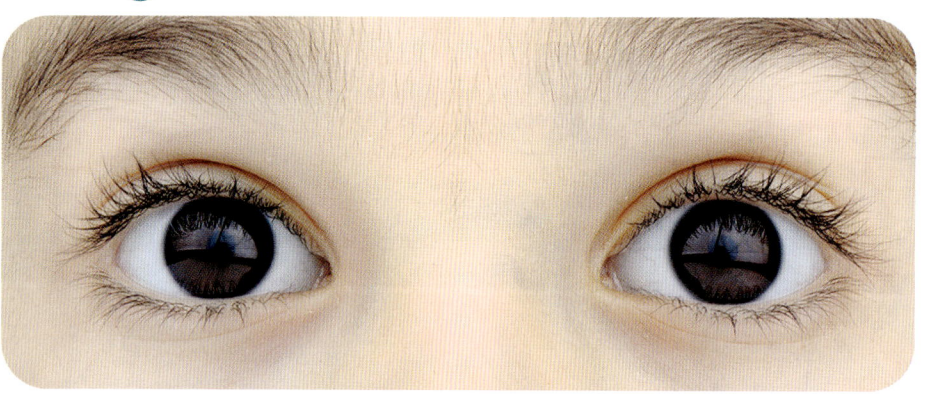

Have you tried to shut out light?

What part of your body do you cover?

Seeing things

Scientists use equipment to help them to see things.

1 Use a magnifying glass to look at your skin.

2 Draw what you see.

3 Now use the magnifying glass to look at some objects in the classroom.

How is a magnifying glass useful?

■ For more activities, go to Workbook 1 page 26.

Hearing

Some things make a sound. Some do not.

Have you ever tried to shut out loud sounds?

What part of your body do you cover?

Investigating sound

1 Try to find an object in your classroom that makes a sound.

2 Use the object to make as many sounds as possible.

3 Listen very carefully to the sounds.

4 Let someone else hear the loudest sound you can make from the object.

Be a scientist

Scientists need to use all of their senses to study the world around them. This is called making observations.

▶ page 9

Key idea

- Our senses help us find out about our world.
- We use our eyes to see. We use our ears to hear.

■ For more activities, go to Workbook 1 page 27.

Our senses: tasting, smelling, touching

In this lesson you will learn about our senses.

Tasting

We use our tongue to taste things. Some food tastes salty and some food tastes sweet.

Our taste can keep us safe. Things that taste bad can sometimes make us ill.

Key words

salty/sweet
senses
smell/smelling
taste/tasting
touch/touching
feeling

Salty or sweet

Look at the different foods.

1 Point to the salty foods.

2 Point to the sweet foods.

What are your favourite foods? Did you all choose the same?

■ For more activities, go to Workbook 1 page 28.

Smelling

Smell is used for many things.

Our sense of smell can keep us safe. It can warn us about things that could make us ill.

Some animals use their strong sense of smell to find food to eat.

Touching

Our sense of touch keeps us safe. When we touch something like a sharp object we can move away quickly before we do too much damage to our body.

Talk about things that smell good to you.

Did you all choose the same?

Look at these photographs.

Point to the things which are dangerous to touch.

What makes it dangerous?

Stretch zone

Look at the photograph. Which of your senses would stop you wanting to eat this food?

Key idea

We have five senses. They are: seeing, hearing, tasting, smelling and touching.

Check how much you know.
Try the puzzles on pages 30–31.

■ For more activities, go to Workbook 1 page 29.

1 Join the dots to make the words.

Now say the words out loud.

2 Draw a line to join the part of the body to its name. One is done for you.

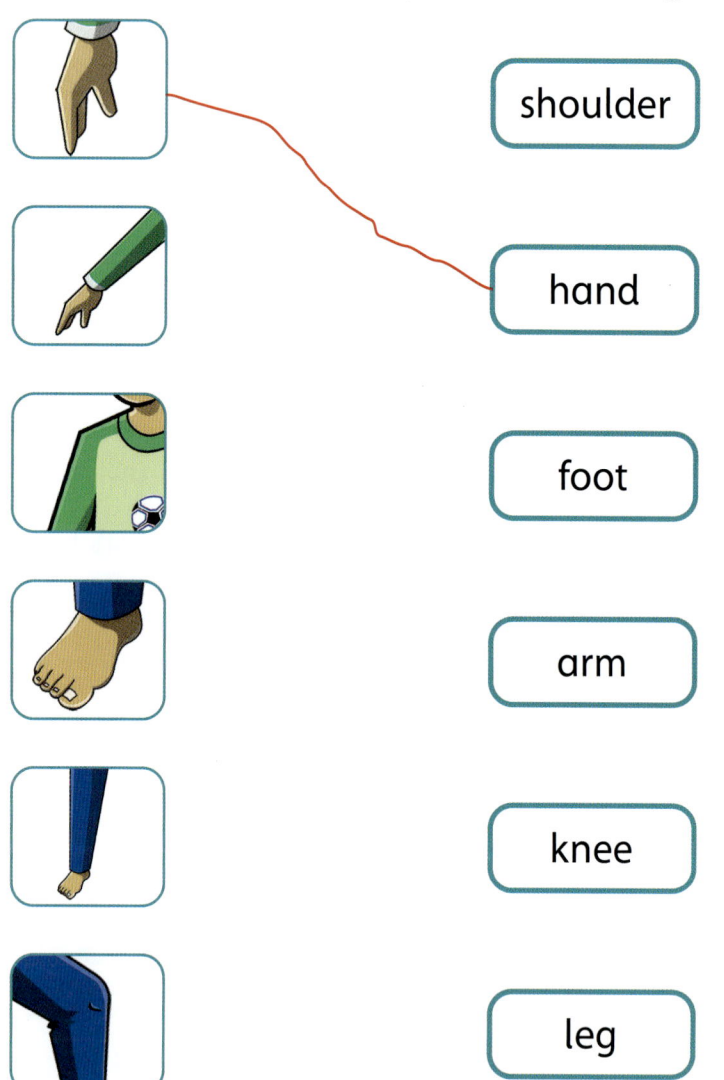

shoulder

hand

foot

arm

knee

leg

3 Tick the one thing that mammals have that birds do not have.

legs ☐   head ☐   eyes ☐   fur ☐

■ For more activities, go to Workbook 1 page 30.

4 Draw a line between each animal and the main group it belongs to.

[vertebrate] [invertebrate]

5 Join the part of the body to the sense. Draw a line.

ears		touch
eyes		hearing
skin		taste
tongue		smell
nose		seeing

6 Circle the correct word to finish each sentence.

I only eat mice. I am a   carnivore   herbivore   omnivore.

I only eat fruit. I am a   carnivore   herbivore   omnivore.

I eat worms and seeds. I am an   carnivore   herbivore   omnivore.

7 A student is investigating the differences in arm length in the class. Which sense does she mainly use to make her measurements?

_____

■ For more activities, go to Workbook 1 page 31.

In this unit you will:

- explore objects and the materials they are made of
- describe what some materials look and feel like
- find out what some materials do
- name some common materials
- sort materials into groups.

Imagine you are holding this toy.

What does it feel like?

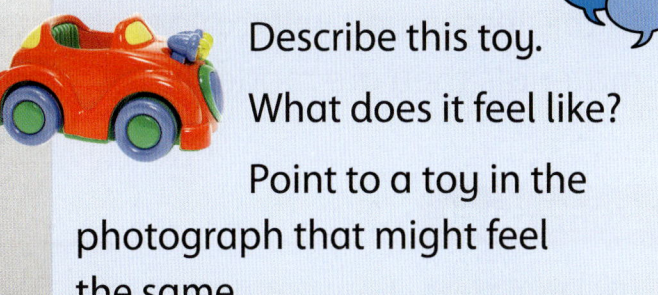

Describe this toy.

What does it feel like?

Point to a toy in the photograph that might feel the same.

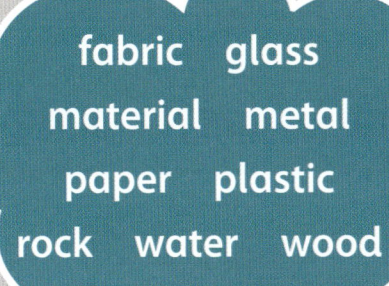

fabric   glass
material   metal
paper   plastic
rock   water   wood

Objects that do the same job can look and feel different.

Look at the toy trains. Can you see any differences?

Science fact

In 2018, scientists from all over the world worked together to make a new material. It is called schwarzite. It is strong but very light.

33

Different materials

In this lesson you will explore objects and the materials they are made of.

Key words
hard/soft
material
object
rough/smooth

Think back

In Unit 1 you learned that we use our senses to find out about objects.

We look at them. We feel them.

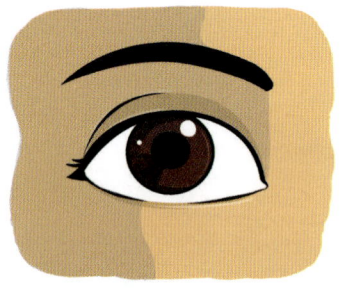 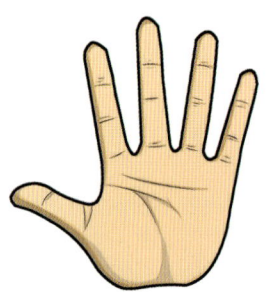

Can you remember the five senses?

Imagine you are touching these objects in a dark room.

How do you know that you are touching the apple and not the wool?

| stone | wooden spoon | balloon | candle |

| apple | paintbrush | wool |

■ For more activities, go to Workbook 1 page 34.

Some objects feel hard. Some objects feel soft.

Look at the different objects on page 34 again.

1 Point to an object that is soft.

2 Point to an object that is hard.

3 Point to an object that is soft and hard.

Objects are made of different materials.

Some materials feel hard.

Other materials feel soft.

Some materials feel smooth.

Other materials feel rough.

Is this object soft or hard? Point to the correct word and say it out loud.

This toy is

soft

hard

What materials can you find?

1 Put your hand inside a bag.

2 Don't look inside. Just feel the objects.

What can you find?

You have used your sense of touch.

Talk to your partner about what each object feels like.

Key idea

• Objects are made of materials.

• Materials look and feel different.

■ For more activities, go to Workbook 1 page 35.

What do materials look and feel like?

In this lesson you will find out what some materials look and feel like.

Key words
dull/shiny
hard/soft
property
rock
rough/smooth

A 'property' means how a material looks. Or what it feels like. Or what it can do.

Look at the objects and the words in the balloons.

1 Point to each object. Say its name out loud.

2 Choose the words from the balloons that describe it.

The red line shows you can use the word 'hard' to describe the rocks.

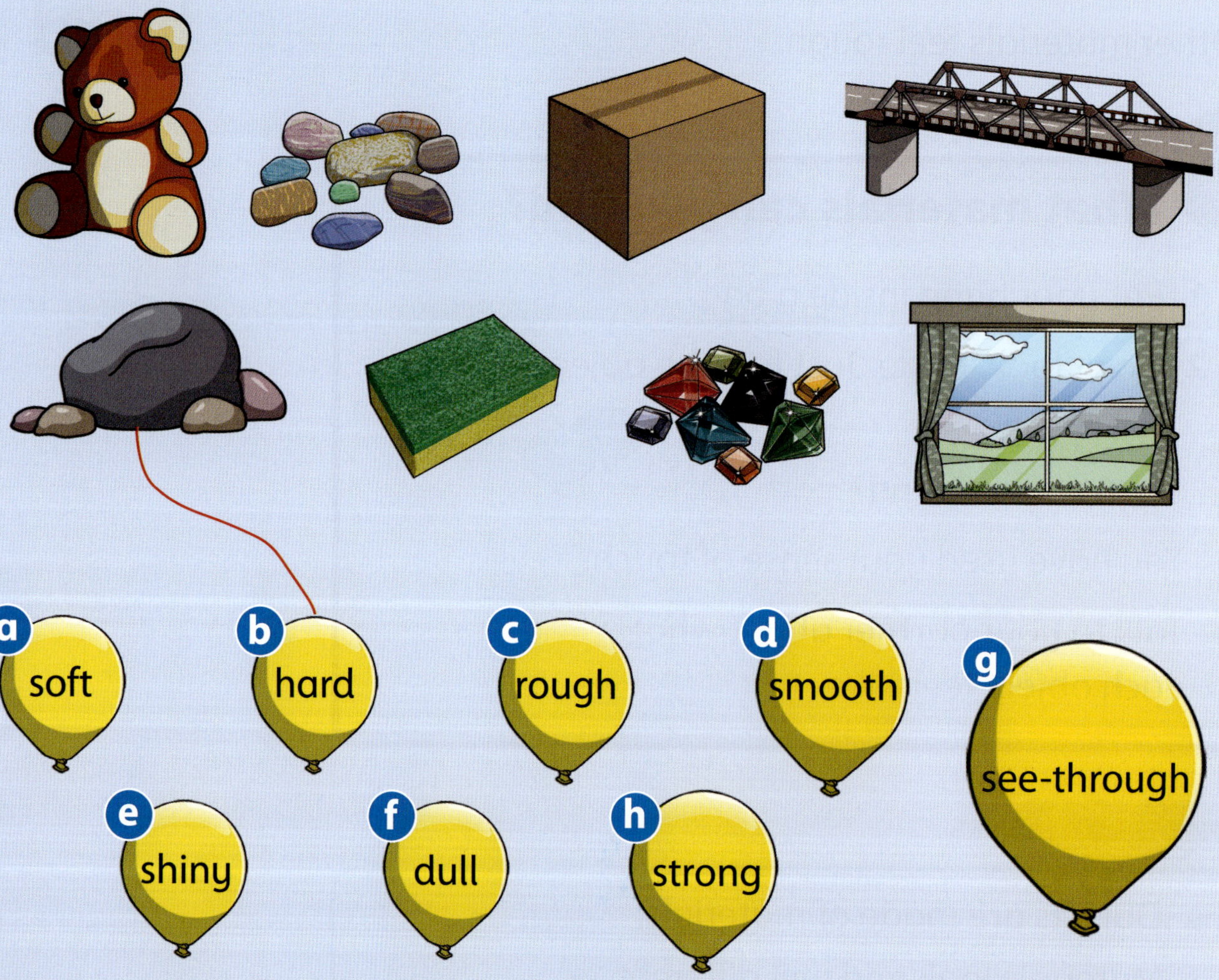

a soft

b hard

c rough

d smooth

e shiny

f dull

g see-through

h strong

36

■ For more activities, go to Workbook 1 page 36.

What is the object like?

1 Find objects in the classroom.
Here are some examples.

What property does each object have?

  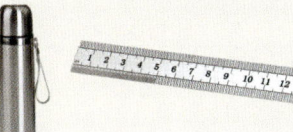  

2 Sort the objects into groups.
Are they hard or soft? Shiny or dull? Rough or smooth?

3 Record what you find. You can use a table like this one.

Object	Hard	Soft	Shiny	Dull	Rough	Smooth
Book	✓			✓		✓

Which object is the hardest?
Which object is the shiniest?
Which object is the smoothest?

Are some objects in more than one group?

Be a scientist

Good scientists record their findings and present their results in tables.
▶ page 10

Science fact

Scientists test how hard materials are by scratching them on other materials.
Diamonds can scratch glass easily.
Diamonds are the hardest natural material.

Key idea

- Materials have different properties.
- They can be hard, soft, shiny, dull, rough or smooth.

2 What is it Made of?

37

■ For more activities, go to Workbook 1 page 37.

What can materials do?

In this lesson you will learn that some materials are waterproof.

Key word
waterproof

If a material keeps water out, it is waterproof.

This child is dry in their raincoat.

What do you have at home that is waterproof?

Which material will keep a person dry in the rain?

Work with your group. Imagine you are going to make an umbrella.

You will need to test some materials.

1 Choose four different materials, such as paper, tin foil, plastic wrap and cloth.

2 Use each material to wrap a ball of cotton wool.

3 Guess which material you think will keep the cotton wool dry. This will be the best material to make an umbrella.

Which material do you think will not make a good umbrella?

Be a scientist
Scientists make guesses based on information they have collected.
This is called a prediction.

▶ page 7

■ For more activities, go to Workbook 1 page 38.

4 Put each cotton wool ball in water. Leave each one for 5 minutes.

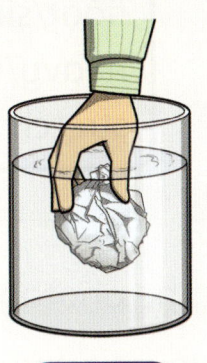

paper

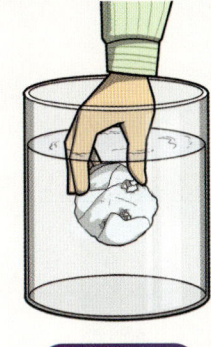

tin foil

plastic wrap

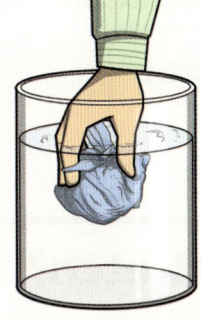

cloth

5 Copy and complete the table. Put a tick under the material that kept the cotton wool the driest.

Paper	Tin foil	Plastic wrap	Cloth

This table shows your results.

Talk in your group about your results.

Did you correctly guess which material is the most waterproof?

Which material is best to make an umbrella? Why?

Have you ever seen an umbrella made from this material?

Key idea

- Some materials keep water out.
- We say they are waterproof.

■ For more activities, go to Workbook 1 page 39.

What else can materials do?

In this lesson you will learn that some materials stretch and some materials can float.

Key words
fabric
float/sink
heavy/light
stretch

Materials that stretch

This person is using a hair band. See how it stretches!

Look at the photograph.

Talk to your partner about it.

Why does the hair band need to stretch?

What material is the hair band made of?

Which materials can stretch?

You are going to investigate some materials.

1 With your partner, look at the objects in the photographs.

2 Guess (predict) which materials will stretch.

3 Test each material to see if your prediction was correct.

Talk about the objects with your partner. Do you know what materials the objects are made of?

■ For more activities, go to Workbook 1 page 40.

Materials can float or sink

Some materials float. This means they can stay on top of water.
Other materials sink. They go below the surface of water.

float

sink

Can you think of a time you saw something sink? Discuss with your partner what material it was made from.

Investigating floating and sinking

You are going to test which materials float in water.

Your teacher will give you and your partner some objects. They will be made out of different materials.

Warning! Be careful because splashed water can make the floor slippery.

1 Predict which objects will float and which will sink. Think about why you make your prediction.

2 Gently place each object onto the water. Let go of the object and observe what happens.

3 Draw the objects. Tick those that float. Draw a line through those that sink.

Were your predictions correct? What helped you to decide if each object would float or sink?

Heavy objects are more likely to sink.
Light objects are more likely to float.

 **Stretch zone**

Why are clothes made of fabric not wood?

Key ideas

- Some materials stretch.
- Some materials float, others sink.

■ For more activities, go to Workbook 1 page 41.

Metals

In this lesson you will discover that metals are useful materials.

Key word
metal

Think back

You learned some words to describe properties of materials earlier in this unit.

1 Point to each word in the box and read it out loud.

2 Talk with your partner about what each word means.

3 Can you think of any objects that the words describe?

4 This bracelet is made of metal. Which words above describe this metal bracelet?

soft
hard
dull
shiny

What are metals like?

Metals are usually hard and shiny.

Metals can be shaped to make different objects.

Metals can be heated up to make them soft. They can be hammered to make shapes. Or stretched to make wire.

Talk with your partner about why this bowl is made of metal.

■ For more activities, go to Workbook 1 page 42.

Metal makes a ringing noise when you hit it.

One metal is not hard. It is liquid, like water.

It is called mercury. It is a dangerous material.

Look for metal objects

1 Look around the classroom.

2 Find objects made of metal.

Do they all have the same properties of metals?

Do they ring?

Are they shiny? Are they hard?

3 Draw the objects you find in your notebook.

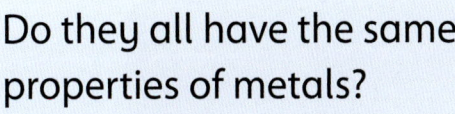

Warning! Be careful when handling metals. They can sometimes be heavy.

Key idea

Metals can be made into lots of different shapes.

2 What is it Made of?

43

■ For more activities, go to Workbook 1 page 43.

Metals and non-metals

In this lesson you will name some materials and sort them into metals or non-metals.

Key word
non-metal

If a material is not a metal we call it a non-metal.

Some common non-metals are plastic, wood, glass, clay pottery, rock and fabric.

clay pottery

wood

plastic

rock

glass

fabric

■ For more activities, go to Workbook 1 page 44.

Is it a metal or a non-metal?

Think back

Use a table of results to record your list, like a scientist does.

Work with a partner to investigate materials.

1 Look at the object your teacher gives you. Is the object metal or non-metal?

2 Think about how you will test to see if the material makes a ringing noise.

3 How will you test if it is shiny or hard?

4 Has it been made into a shape?

5 Now look for other objects around your school. In your notebook, make a list or draw pictures of what you find.

6 Tick the non-metal objects.

Tell your teacher and the other people in your class about your results.

2 What is it Made of?

Stretch zone

How do you know if an object is made of plastic or wood?

Key idea

Materials are either metals or non-metals.

45

Useful materials

In this lesson you will name some useful materials.

Think back

Think of some objects you have used so far in this unit. What did you use them for? Why?

Talk to your partner about why you think bridges are made from metal and not paper.

We can name some common materials.

These are the ones that we use the most.

Wood is very common.

Which one of these objects is normally made of wood?

What is the other object normally made of?

a b

46

■ For more activities, go to Workbook 1 page 46.

Plastic and glass are also used to make a lot of objects.

tumbler

alarm clock

spoon

door

glasses

hair brush

Look at the photographs.

1 Tell your partner two things we use glass for.

2 Name two things in the photographs made of plastic.

3 What do you use that is made of glass?

Key idea

Some materials are so important we use them a lot.

47

Sorting materials into groups

In this lesson you will sort materials into groups.

Key words
compare
groups
sort

Rubber can be stretchy or bouncy.

It is always waterproof.

rubber balls   rubber boots

rubber bands   rubber gloves

Science fact

We get natural rubber from rubber trees. The liquid rubber is collected by cutting into the bark.

Talk about the photographs with your partner.

Point to each of the names and read them out loud.

Can you match the names to the objects?

Talk about why you think rubber is used to make these objects.

48

■ For more activities, go to Workbook 1 page 48.

Grouping materials

1 Your teacher will give you some objects made from different materials. Use two sorting circles or hoops to compare and sort them.

You can use the photographs below as one example of sorting.

2 Put each group inside a sorting circle.

 Stretch zone

Why is grouping objects by colour not scientific?

Objects are often made from more than one material. Look at this bicycle and answer the questions using the words in the box.

What is the handle made of?

What is the frame made of?

What is the tyre made of?

| metal | plastic | rubber |

Check how much you know.
Try the puzzles on pages 50–51.

Key idea

We can compare and sort materials into groups, like families.

■ For more activities, go to Workbook 1 page 49.

What have I learned about materials?

1 Circle two objects that are made of metal.

2 Here are four properties of materials.

Write out the words in full.

s _ f _   d _ _ l   h _ r _   s _ _ _ y

3

sink

float

a Draw a line from the correct word to describe what is happening to the apple.

b Draw a line from the correct word to describe what is happening to the spoon.

■ For more activities, go to Workbook 1 page 50.

4 Here are four non-metals. Write out the words in full.

Draw a line from each word to match it to the correct photograph.

p _ p _ r   r _ b _ _ r

f _ b _ _ c   w _ _ d

5 Circle the best answer.

a Pans are made of metal because

they need to be shiny.   they need to let heat through.

b Pans are not made of paper because

paper is not shiny.   paper will catch fire.

 **6**

Complete the table to record the properties of these objects. One has been done for you.

Object	Hard	Soft	Shiny	Dull	Rough	Smooth
Book	✓			✓		✓
Cushion						
Pencil						

■ For more activities, go to Workbook 1 page 51.

3 Pushes and Pulls

In this unit you will:

- explore and describe movement

- understand that pushes and pulls are forces

- learn what makes things speed up, slow down or change direction.

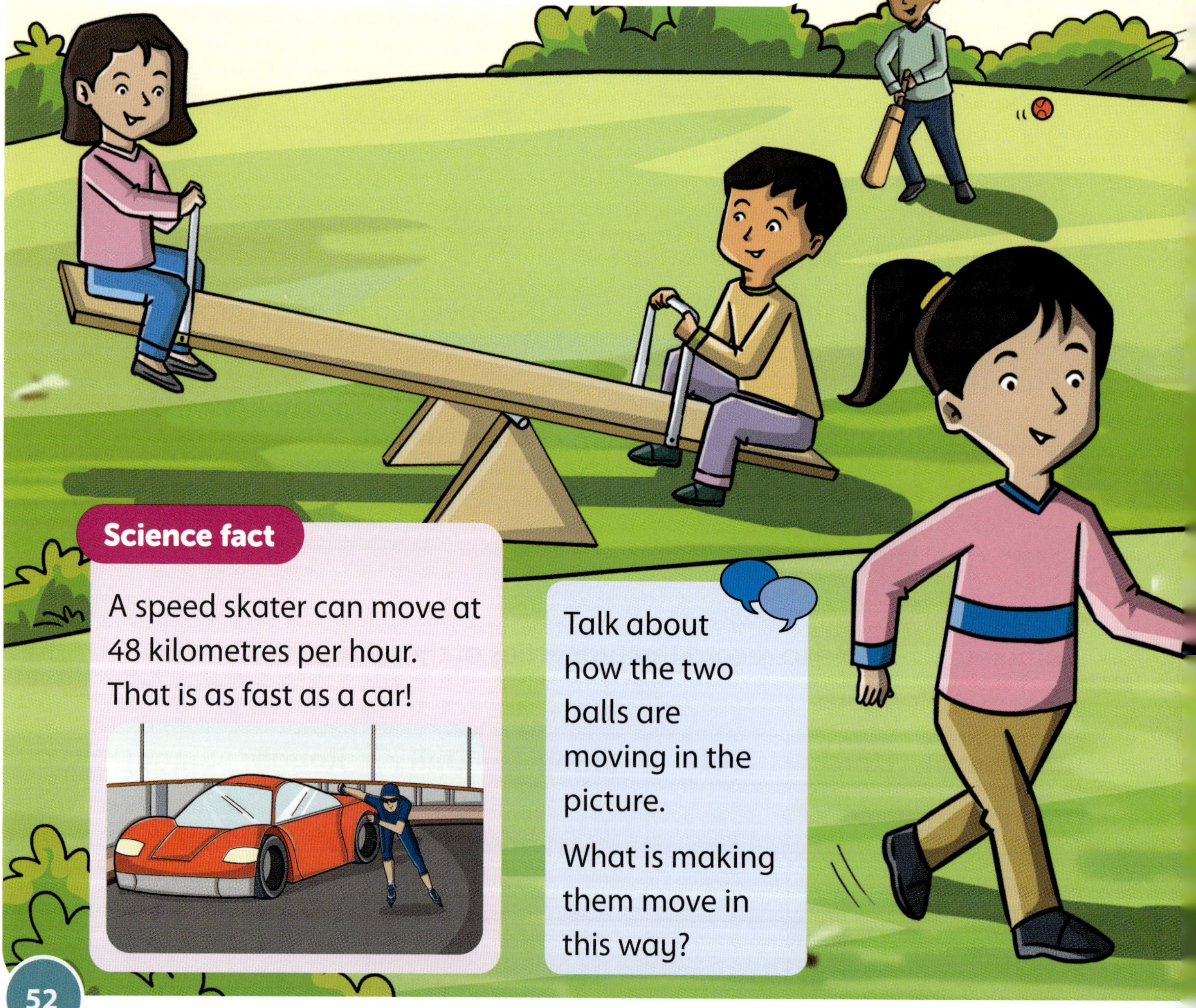

Science fact

A speed skater can move at 48 kilometres per hour. That is as fast as a car!

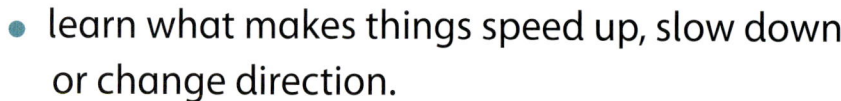

Talk about how the two balls are moving in the picture.

What is making them move in this way?

■ For more activities, go to Workbook 1 pages 52–53.

Stopping and starting

In this lesson you will learn that forces can make things move and stop things moving.

Key words
forces
move

Some of the cars in the photograph are moving.

Some of the cars have stopped.

Forces can make things move.

Forces can also stop things moving.

Can you see any flags moving?

What is making the flags move?

Which way are they moving?

The flags are not going anywhere.

They stay on the flagpole and they move backwards and forwards in the wind.

 Stretch zone

Why do some things move in the wind but others do not?

■ For more activities, go to Workbook 1 page 54.

How many different ways can you move your body?

Runners start in this position. They push their feet away from the ground so that they can start running quickly.

How do we move?

1 Think about when you walk. How do your legs move? Do you swing your arms?

Your teacher will take you to a safe open space.

2 Try to copy the starting position of the runners in the picture.

3 Now stand up straight and start to run.

Your teacher will show you the finish line.

4 Use your best starting position to run as fast as you can to the finish line.

Talk to a partner about how you started to run.

Does the starting position help you to move quicker?

Talk to your partner about how you stopped. Did you slow down before you stopped?

 Stretch zone

What do you think would happen if you just stopped your feet moving when you were running quickly?

Key idea

Forces help things to move and stop.

3 Pushes and Pulls

55

■ For more activities, go to Workbook 1 page 55.

Look at things moving in wind

In this lesson you will learn what makes things speed up, slow down or change direction.

Key words
direction
slow down/
speed up

The wind is blowing the sand away from the hand.

The wind makes leaves in the trees move.

Look at the photograph.

Is the sand falling straight down?

Why not?

Science fact

Turbines use wind to make electricity. The largest wind turbine in the world is in Hawaii. It has blades the length of a football field.

Talk about how the wind turbine moves. What makes its blades move?

■ For more activities, go to Workbook 1 page 56.

Make a paper windmill

Work with a partner and help each other.

1 Cut a piece of square paper, as shown.

2 Take each corner and overlap them at the centre hole. Help each other to do this.

3 Hold all the corners in place with a paper fastener.

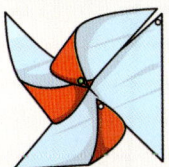

4 Wrap the ends of the paper fastener around the stick. Put some tape over the stick to hold it in place.

5 Blow your windmill.

Talk to your partner. Decide what the missing words are using the word box below.

When I blow hard, the windmill moves

f a s t e r.

When I blow softly, the windmill moves

_ _ _ _ _ _.

The windmill

_ _ _ _ _

round and round, but it does not move to another

_ _ _ _ _.

moves	slower
~~faster~~	place

Key idea

The wind can make things go faster and change direction.

■ For more activities, go to Workbook 1 page 57.

Look at things moving in water and wind

In this lesson you will learn what causes things to move.

Key words
move
speed up/
slow down

A sailboat uses the wind to move.

Science fact

Racing sailboats can move at speeds of up to 28 kilometres per hour. That's pretty fast.

Racing a sailing boat

Your teacher will give you a model sailing boat.

1 Float the boat in a water tray.

Pretend to be the wind. Blow on the boat to make it move.

Make the boat start, speed up, slow down and stop, using your breath.

2 Take it in turns to make the boat move.

Who can make the boat move the fastest?

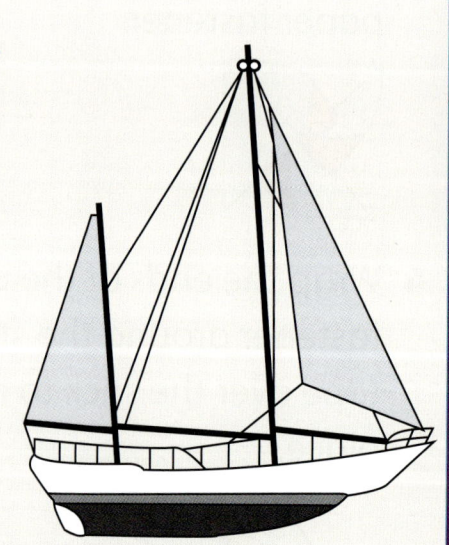

Stretch zone

Was it harder to make the boat start or to make it stop?

■ For more activities, go to Workbook 1 page 58.

This boy is pouring some water into the toy waterwheel.

Can you describe how the water is making the wheel move?

What happens when the boy stops pouring the water?

Predict what happens if the boy pours lots of water in.

How do bubbles move in the wind?

1 Use some bubble liquid and a wand to blow bubbles.

2 Predict what will happen to the bubbles.

What makes the bubbles move in this way?

Why do the bubbles change direction?

When do they move faster?

When do they slow down?

Be a scientist

When you predict something you guess what is most likely to happen.

▶ page 7

Key idea

Water and wind can make things move.

3 Pushes and Pulls

59

Explore how things move (pushes and pulls)

In this lesson you will look at how things move.

Key words
forces
move
push/pull

We cannot see forces. But they make things move.

Looking at a moving ball

1 Sit opposite your partner. Push the ball to your partner.

2 Now pull the ball back to you.

What happens to the ball?

Talk with your partner. How is the ball moving? What is movement?

Be a scientist

Scientists look closely to find out about the world. This is called observation.

▶ page 9

Forces are making objects move all the time.

Finding moving things

1 Look around the classroom. Find things that are moving.

2 Predict whether a push, a pull or both are making the things move.

3 Then write what you see in a table like the one below.

Object moving	Describe the movement	Push, pull or push and pull?
Ball rolling	The ball is rolling across the floor.	Push

Your teacher will tell you the correct force for each movement you wrote down. Was this what you predicted?

■ For more activities, go to Workbook 1 page 60.

Indoor bowling using pushes and pulls

1 Line up 10 empty water bottles.

2 Take turns to pull a ball back and then push it towards the bottles.

3 Who can knock the most bottles down using only one push?

4 How many pushes does it take to knock all of the bottles down?

Warning! Push the ball along the floor. Do not throw it or you could hurt someone.

Look at the picture of children playing games.

Point to a person using a push force.

Point to a person using a pull force.

Key idea

Pushes and pulls are forces.

■ For more activities, go to Workbook 1 page 61.

Fast and slow-moving objects

In this lesson you will understand that pushes and pulls can make things move faster and slower.

Some vehicles move much slower than others.

Some vehicles move much faster than others.

What happens to the forces to make the cars move faster?

Looking at the movement of traffic

Your teacher will take you outside to look at the traffic.

1 Can you see any vehicles speeding up?

2 Can you see any vehicles slowing down?

3 Can you see any vehicles that have stopped?

Warning! Listen to and stay near your teacher when you are near the road.

■ For more activities, go to Workbook 1 page 62.

Making a ramp for toy cars

1 Work with a partner to make a ramp using books.

2 Make the toy car move up the ramp. What force did you use to move the toy car up the ramp?

3 Now move the toy car along a flat surface. What force did you use?

4 Is it harder to move the toy car up the ramp or on the flat surface?

5 Now move the toy car down the ramp. Don't let it go.

What force did you use to move the toy car down the ramp?

6 When did the car move faster? Point to your answer.

| up a hill down a hill flat surface |

7 When did the car move slower?
Point to your answer.

| up a hill down a hill flat surface |

Warning!
Don't push the car very hard or it may hurt someone.

Stretch zone

What might happen if you used a bigger, heavier car?

Key idea

Forces can make objects move faster or slower.

■ For more activities, go to Workbook 1 page 63.

Exploring the movement of toys

In this lesson you will make and watch moving things.

Key words
faster/slower
move

You can use forces to make toys move.

Make a toy car

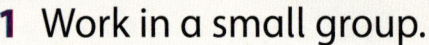

1 Work in a small group.

2 Think about how to make a moving toy from card or wood.

You will need some wheels.

What
different ways
can toys move?

How could you make it even better?

Make a balloon toy car

1 Fix a balloon to the toy car you made.

2 Put a straw in the balloon.

3 Hold the end of the straw between your fingers.

4 Carefully blow up the balloon.

5 When you let go, the air from the balloon pushes the toy car forward.

What forces move the toy car?

Warning!
Only blow up your own balloon.

■ For more activities, go to Workbook 1 page 64.

Testing a bouncy toy

Your teacher will give you a toy made from a spring.

1 Stretch the spring and let it go.

 What force moves the bouncy toy?

2 Some toys use a key to wind the toy up.

 What force do you use when you use the key?

Warning! Be careful not to over stretch the spring. It could spring back into your face.

Classroom hunt for moving toys

1 Work with a partner to find moving toys in your classroom.

2 Choose one toy. Talk about how the toy moves.

> How could you make the toy move faster? How could you make it slow down? How could you make it stop?

Check how much you know.
Try the puzzles on pages 66–67.

Key idea

We can make moving toys.

■ For more activities, go to Workbook 1 page 65.

1 Here are some ways you can move your body.

Draw a line to the correct word that matches each picture.

spinning   swinging

hopping   walking

2 What is moving the things in these pictures?

Circle the correct word under each picture.

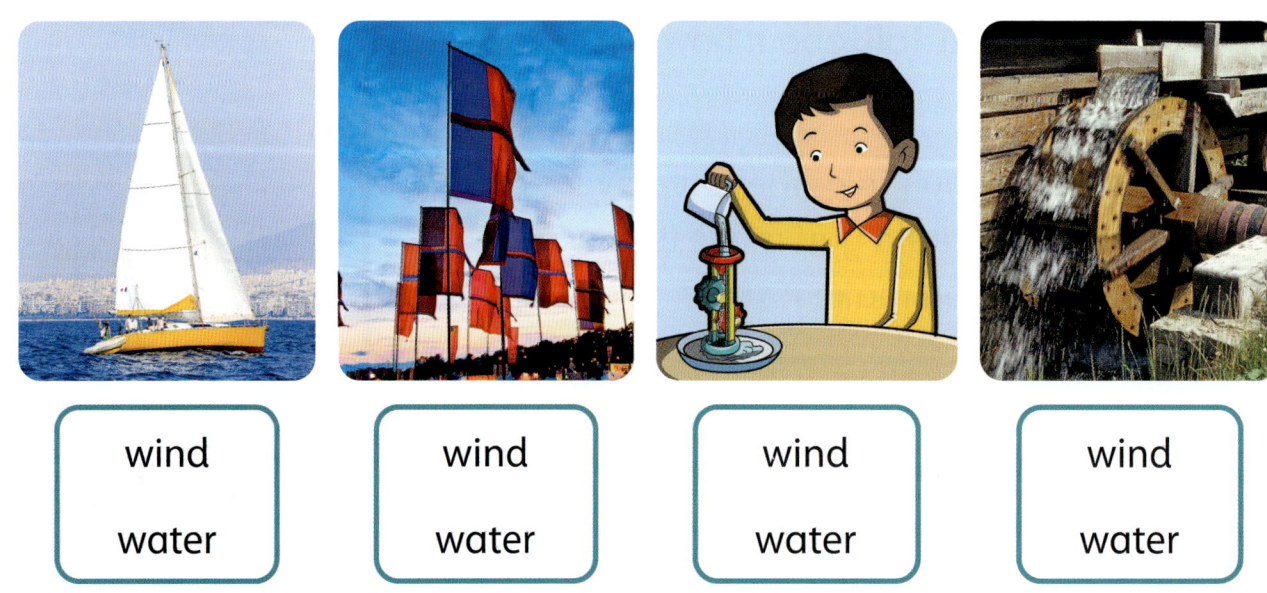

wind	wind	wind	wind
water	water	water	water

■ For more activities, go to Workbook 1 page 66.

3 How can you make these toys move? Underline the correct answer.

You might need to underline more than one word for some toys.

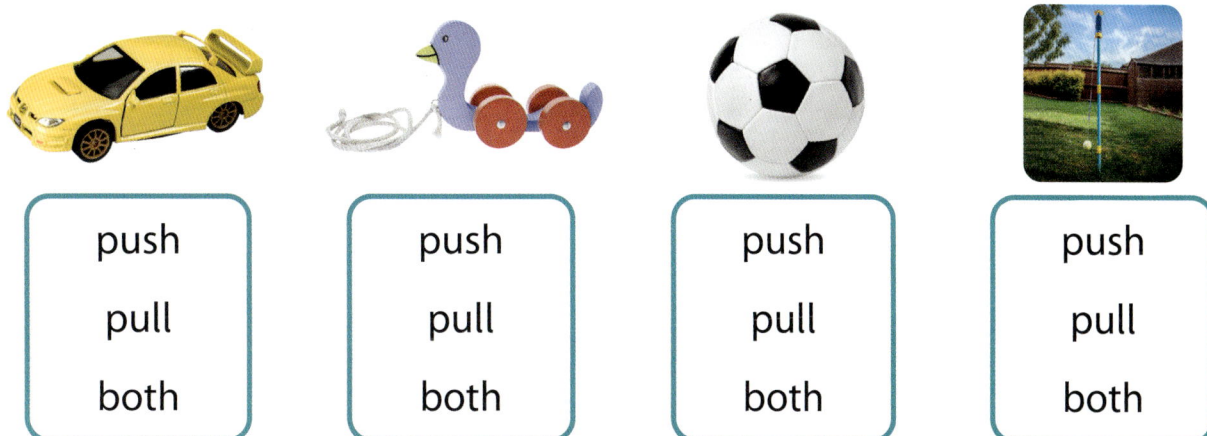

push	push	push	push
pull	pull	pull	pull
both	both	both	both

4 Write in the correct words for each sentence from the word box.

Forces can make things m _ _ _.

Forces can also s _ _ _ things moving.

P _ _ _ _ _ and P _ _ _ _ are f _ r _ _ s.

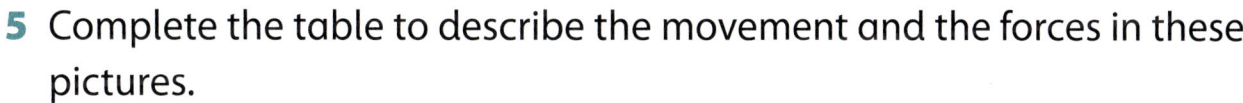

forces   pulls   pushes   move   stop

5 Complete the table to describe the movement and the forces in these pictures.

Object moving	Describe the movement	Push, pull or push and pull?
Ball being thrown		
Car rolling		
Playing bowling		

■ For more activities, go to Workbook 1 page 67.

4 Making Sounds

In this unit you will:

- name some of the sources of sound
- explore what happens to sounds when we move about
- understand that our ears hear sounds.

Talk about what the children are doing in the photograph.

What do you think their audience is doing?

What sounds do you think these children are making?

What are they using to make the sounds?

loud   quiet
sound   voice

Science fact

Some animals, like sea sponges, do not make sounds.

Help

Who do you think is making the loudest sound? Who is making the quietest sound?

■ For more activities, go to Workbook 1 pages 68–69.

Talking and listening

In this lesson you will find out about the sources of sound.

Key words
sound
voice

We can make many sounds with our voices.
Lots of animals make sounds.

Look at the picture.

Can you point to where sounds are being made?

Can you make the same sounds using your voice?

Sitting in silence

1 In your group try to sit quietly and not talk.

   How many minutes did you not talk for?

2 Talk to the rest of the class about how this felt.

Think about why we talk to each other.

Can you imagine not talking?

We talk to each other to share ideas.

Some animals make noises to warn of danger.

Or to frighten other animals that might hurt them.

■ For more activities, go to Workbook 1 page 70.

Humans and other animals can sing.

Birds sing to pass on information.

People sing for lots of different reasons.

Do you know any songs that you could hum to the others in your group?

Take it in turns to hum a song to the group. Did they recognise the song?

Why do we sing?

Key idea

Animals and humans talk and listen to each other.

Science fact

Some people cannot fully hear all sounds. This affects about 1 in 20 people.

■ For more activities, go to Workbook 1 page 71.

Making sounds

In this lesson you will learn that we can use our body to make sounds.

Key words
loud/quiet

We make lots of sounds with our body.

Some sports people whistle to get the attention of the other players.

Other people whistle because it is good fun.

They whistle along to music.

Science fact

Humans can use a special whistle that only dogs and some cats can hear.

What is the child doing?

Why do you think people do this?

What sounds can you make?

You are going to make different sounds with your body.

1 Try to whistle. Purse your lips together and then gently blow.
  Can you whistle a tune?

2 Clap your hands together.
  Clap hard and then gently to make different sounds.

3 Listen to the clapping rhythm your teacher makes.
  Can you copy it?

When do people clap?

What happens when you clap hard? What happens when you clap gently?

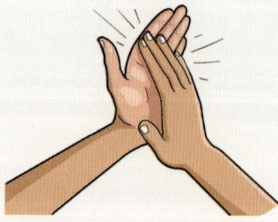

72

■ For more activities, go to Workbook 1 page 72.

Animal sounds

Choose an animal from the pictures. Make the sound it makes.

Can your partner match the sound to the picture?

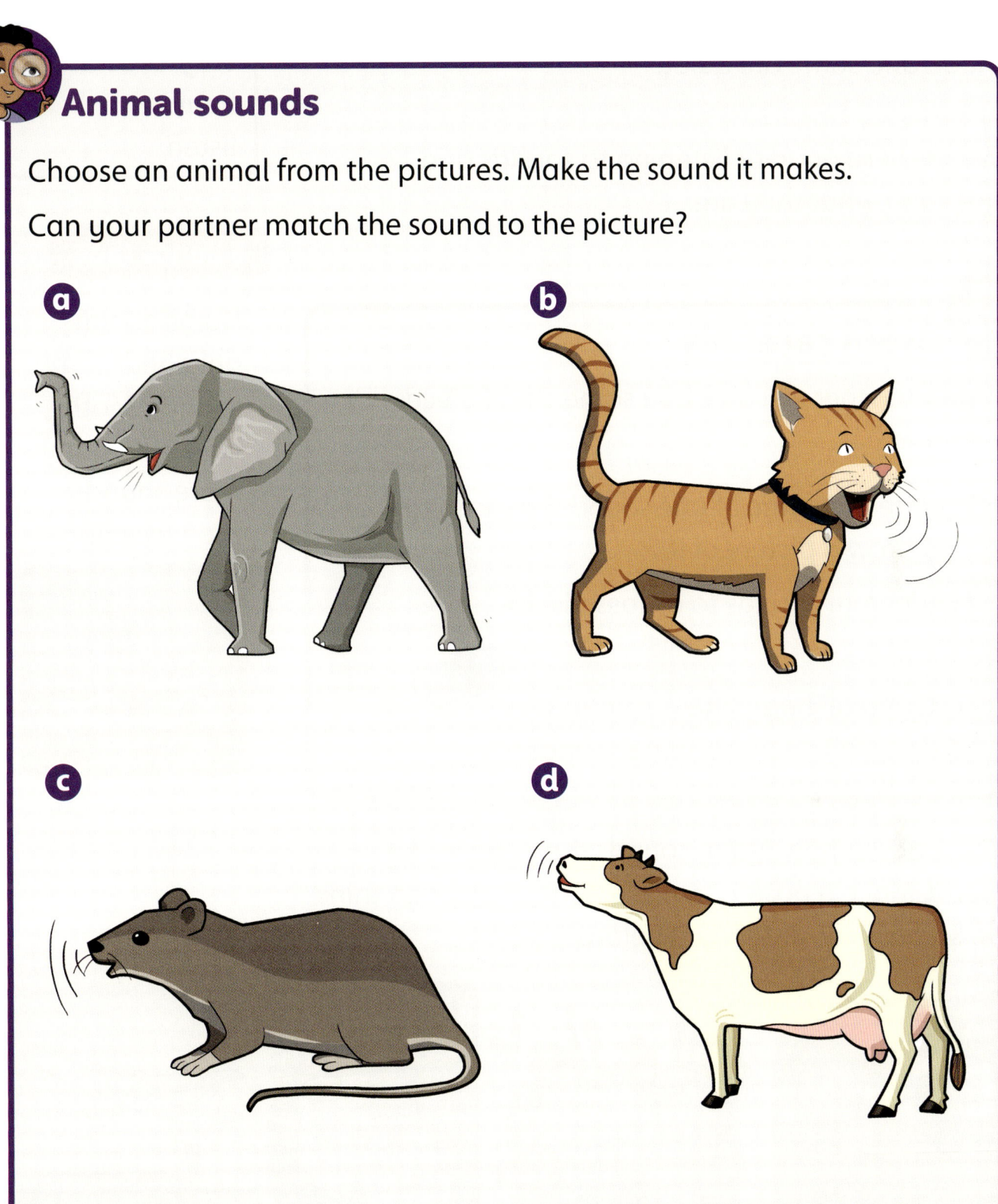

a

b

c

d

Key idea

We use our body to make sounds.

■ For more activities, go to Workbook 1 page 73.

Quiet and loud sounds

In this lesson you will learn that some sounds are loud and some are quiet.

Key words
hear
listen

We are very good at listening to sounds and guessing what they are.

Listen carefully

Your teacher will give you some small pieces of card.

1 Write the name of one sound that you can hear or draw a picture of it.

2 Add your sounds to a class display.

Did you all hear different sounds or did you all hear the same sounds?

Science fact

Humans can only hear some sounds. Moths can hear many more sounds than we can.

Think about how many sounds there are in the world. Make a poster of all the sounds you can think of. Some ideas are shown below.

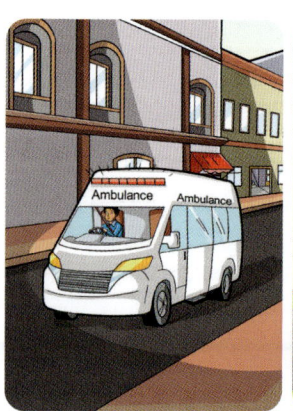

■ For more activities, go to Workbook 1 page 74.

Some sounds can be loud, for example, a siren. Some sounds can be quiet, for example, a butterfly flying.

Describing sounds in school

Go on a listening walk around the school.

1 Predict what you think the loudest sound will be.

2 Predict what you think the quietest sound will be.

3 Listen to the sounds you hear. Are they loud, quiet or both?

Tell your teacher when you hear a sound. Write down your sounds in a table of results like this one.

Sound	Quiet, Loud or Both

Did anyone hear anything different?

How many sounds did the whole group hear?

 Stretch zone

Compare your predictions with the results in your table. Do they agree?

 **Be a scientist**

Scientists can measure and record sounds using a special bit of equipment called a sound meter.

▶ page 8

Key idea

Sounds can be quiet, loud, or both.

4 Making Sounds

75

■ For more activities, go to Workbook 1 page 75.

Sounds and moving about

In this lesson you will explore how sounds change when we move closer to them or further away from them.

Think back

Do you remember the listening walk? You had to listen very carefully to hear some of the sounds.

Listen to your teacher walking away from you.

What happens to the sound when your teacher moves further away?

What happens to the sound when your teacher moves closer again?

When we move further away from where a sound is made, does the sound get quieter?

You can investigate this by playing a game.

■ For more activities, go to Workbook 1 page 76.

What happens to sounds when we get further away from them?

Predict what will happen to a sound when you get further away from it.

1 Go outside into a big open space.

One person stands in the centre with their eyes closed.

They are the Listener.

2 Stand in a circle around the Listener.

Stand as far away as possible.

3 Tiptoe very quietly towards the Listener.

The Listener listens very carefully.

If they hear a sound, they turn around quickly and open their eyes.

If they see you moving, you must go back to the start. See who gets to the centre first.

Were some of you quieter than others? Why?

Be a scientist

Scientists ask questions and listen carefully to the answers. This helps them to work out solutions to difficult problems.

▶ page 7

Key idea

Sounds change when we move closer to them or further away from them.

■ For more activities, go to Workbook 1 page 77.

Sounds around us

In this lesson you will discover the importance of quiet and loud sounds.

Key words
loud/quiet

Think back

Do you remember the listening walk? You had to listen very carefully to hear some of the sounds.

Wild animals have quiet feet.

Animals that hunt have very quiet feet!

Look at the photograph of the leopard paw. Their feet have soft pads. This is so they can creep up on other animals.

Padded leopard paw

They try to get as close as they can before the other animal hears them. Just like you did in the game you played on the last page.

Hyena creeps up on prey

Imagine you are in the jungle. You want to creep up on an animal. What shoes would you wear? Why?

Moving quietly

1 Your teacher will give you some items to investigate.

Can you make some special shoes to help you move quietly?

■ For more activities, go to Workbook 1 page 78.

2 Choose a pair to put on your feet.

Do they make you move quieter or louder?

Which ones would you wear to creep up on an animal?

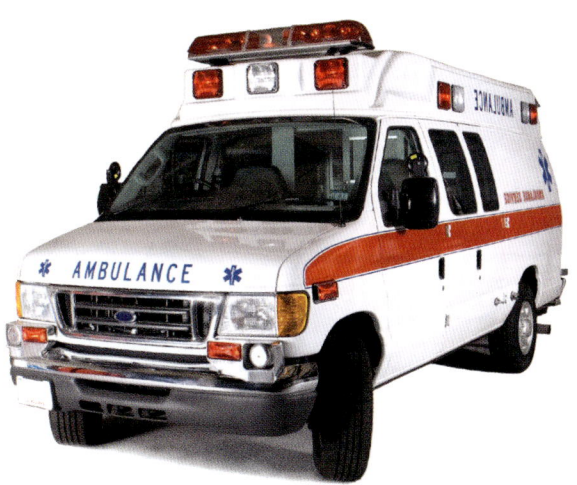

The sirens let people know that there could be danger.

They also let people know that help is coming.

On busy roads other drivers hear the siren and can move out of the way.

Talk to your partner about what emergency vehicles you know. Can you name any?

Why do these vehicles need sirens?

Key idea

- Some animals can move very quietly.
- Some vehicles are very loud.

Stretch zone

What happens to the sound of a car when it is moving nearer to you?

4 Making Sounds

79

■ For more activities, go to Workbook 1 page 79.

How we hear sounds

In this lesson you will discover that we use our ears to hear sounds.

Key words
ear
hear

Sound travels from the place where it is made, into our ears.

We hear when sound travels into the ear.

We have two ears to help us hear sounds all around us.

Can you hear with only one ear?

1 Sit quietly and close your eyes.

2 Put your hand over one ear. Listen.

3 Now take your hand away from your ear. Listen again.

4 Cover your other ear and listen.

Can you hear the same sounds? Are there some sounds you can hear better than others, such as quieter sounds or louder sounds?

5 Predict what would happen if you covered both of your ears.

Sit in a safe place and try this.

Did you predict correctly?

Are two ears better than one?

Talk about how we hear things.

Point to the part of the body that we use to hear things. Say the name out loud.

80

■ For more activities, go to Workbook 1 page 80.

Eyes and hearing?

1 Your teacher will make a sound. Listen to this carefully.

2 Now close your eyes and listen to the sound again.

3 Can you hear the sound clearer with your eyes open or closed?

 Stretch zone ➤

Do you think our eyes and ears work together?

About 70 million people in the world use a language called sign language to communicate.

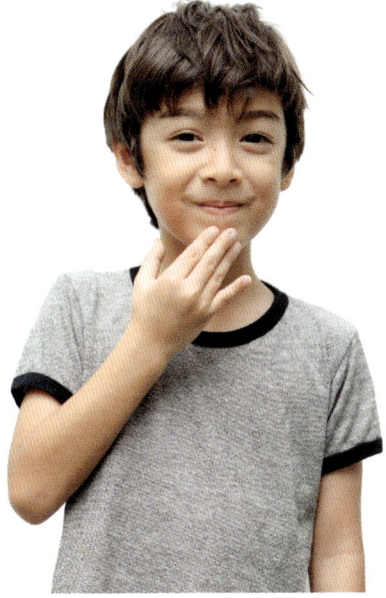

This child is signing 'thank you'.

Check how much you know.
Try the puzzles on pages 82–83.

Key idea

We use our ears to hear sounds.

■ For more activities, go to Workbook 1 page 81.

1 Tick the photograph that would be quieter.

2 Underline the correct answer in each of these sentences.

We hear sounds through our   eyes / ears.

Sounds from further away are   quieter / louder.

Sounds closer to us are   quieter / louder.

This vehicle has a   loud / quiet siren.

■ For more activities, go to Workbook 1 page 82.

3 Humans and animals make sounds for different reasons.
What are they? Use the words in the box to complete the sentences.

To **w** _ _ _
of danger.

To **f r** _ _ _ _ _ **e n**
other animals.

To **p** _ _ **s**
on information.

frighten   pass   warn

4 Which two senses are most important when we cross the road?
Circle the correct pictures.

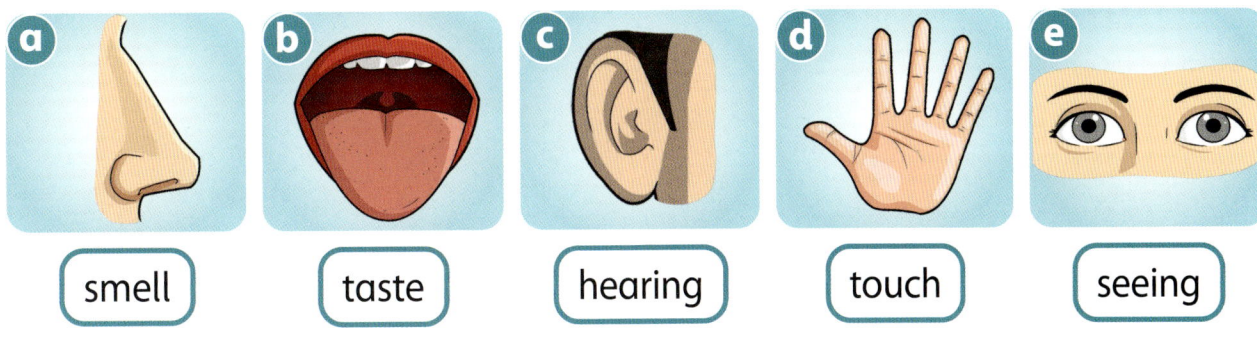

| a smell | b taste | c hearing | d touch | e seeing |

5 Which piece of equipment does a scientist use to measure sound
accurately?

_____

■ For more activities, go to Workbook 1 page 83.

5 Plants and the Seasons

In this unit you will:

- name the main parts of plants and trees
- find and name wild plants and garden plants
- observe changes across the seasons
- describe weather and day length in different seasons.

Look at the plants. Which parts of them can you name? Talk about some of the different plants you can see. Can you name their parts?

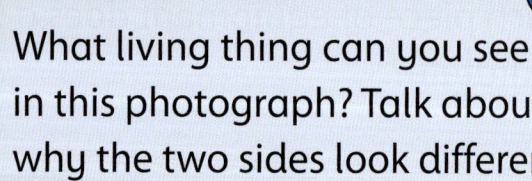

What living thing can you see in this photograph? Talk about why the two sides look different.

flower
leaf plant roots
season stem
trunk wild

Science fact

There are thousands of different types of plants on Earth. We use many of them for food and shelter.

What is the weather like in this photograph?
What other types of weather do you know?

■ For more activities, go to Workbook 1 pages 84–85.

Parts of a plant

In this lesson you will name the major parts of a plant.

Key words
flower
leaves
roots
stem

Plants have four main parts:

- the roots
- the leaves
- the stem
- the flower.

Look at this plant and read the labels.

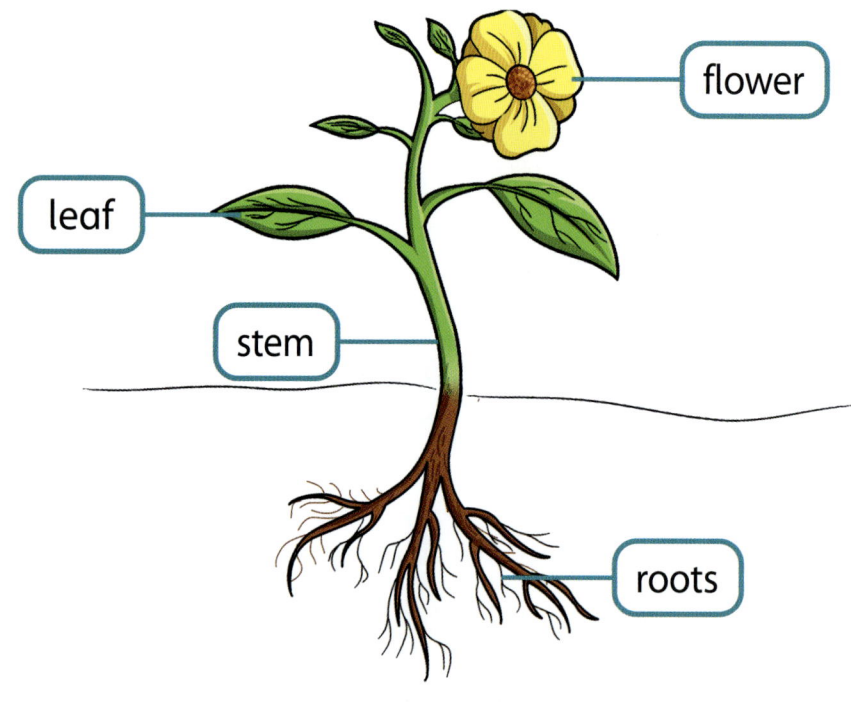

Finding the parts of a plant

Look at the plant your teacher has given you.

1 Study any flowers. What colour are they?

2 Find the roots. How long are they?

3 Count the leaves. How many are there?

4 Look at the stem. Does it bend easily?

5 Draw your plant and label the parts.

Display your plant picture.

■ For more activities, go to Workbook 1 page 86.

We can eat parts of plants.

1 Look at these photographs. Write the name of each plant in your notebook. Use the words in the box to help you.

a  **b**  **c**  **d**

carrots   celery   lettuce   saffron flower

2 Point to the right word to match the description of the food to the correct photograph. The first one is shown by the red line.

When we eat lettuce we are eating the

When we eat carrots we are eating the

When we eat celery we are eating the

When we eat saffron we are eating part of the

Many plants are good to eat because they help to keep us healthy.

roots

leaves

flower

stem

 Warning! Some plants can make us very ill. They are not good to eat.

Stretch zone

Name two other plants that you eat.

Which parts do you eat?

■ For more activities, go to Workbook 1 page 87.

Key idea

We can eat some parts of some plants: stem, flower, root, leaf.

Looking at wild and garden plants

In this lesson you will find and name plants and trees.

Key words

deciduous

evergreen

stem

trees

trunk

Some trees are flowering plants. Trees have a woody stem in the middle. This is called a trunk.

Trees are much bigger than flowers. Shrubs are also bigger than flowers. Shrubs are smaller than trees and have many stems.

Look at the picture of the forest. Point to the flowers, shrubs and trees.

In your group, talk about the plants you have seen before. Decide which are flowers, which are shrubs and which are trees.

Science fact

Some trees never lose their leaves. These are called evergreen trees. Trees that lose their leaves are called deciduous trees.

88

■ For more activities, go to Workbook 1 page 88.

Survey of flowering plants

You will visit a garden and a wild place, such as a forest.

1 With a partner, look for any examples of flowers, shrubs and trees in both places. Draw or take photographs of them.

2 Make a scrapbook of your drawings or photographs.

In one section, show the plants you found in the garden.

In the second section, show the plants you found in the wild place.

> How were the plants in the garden different from the plants in the wild place?

Investigating trees

1 Look at three different trees near your school.

2 Make a leaf rubbing from each tree. Use this as the centre of an information card about each tree.

3 Measure how wide the trunk is. Write this on the card.

4 Identify any trees that lose their leaves. Write this on the card.

5 Draw each tree on its information card.

Be a scientist

Scientists measure very carefully so that results are correct.

▶ page 9

Key idea

There are many types of plants in your area. These can be flowers, shrubs or trees.

■ For more activities, go to Workbook 1 page 89.

Weather

In this lesson you will observe and find out about the weather.

Key words
cloudy
day
rain
snow
sunny
symbols
weather
windy

Look at the pictures. With a partner, talk about these different types of weather.

Which types of weather have you seen where you live?

The different types of weather are given symbols. You may have seen these while watching TV weather forecasts.

Point to the symbol to link it with the name of the weather it shows.

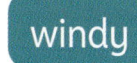 sunny    windy    snow   cloudy   rain

■ For more activities, go to Workbook 1 page 90.

Observing weather

1 Observe the weather at the same time every day for five days.

2 Write down what you see.

You could use a table like the one below.

	Day 1	Day 2	Day 3	Day 4	Day 5	Prediction for day 6	Day 6
Weather symbol							

3 What do you think the weather will be like on day 6? This is your prediction.

4 Observe the weather on day 6 to see if your prediction was correct.

Scientists who study the weather are called meteorologists.

They use new technologies such as satellites to gather information about the weather.

Stretch zone

Research in books or on the internet to find out where the hottest, coldest, driest and wettest parts of the world are.

How does your region compare? Share your findings with the class.

Key idea

There are different types of weather around the world.

■ For more activities, go to Workbook 1 page 91.

The seasons

In this lesson you will observe the changes in weather and the length of day across the seasons.

Key words
autumn
season
spring
summer
winter

The weather and day length can change over a year.

Summer is the hottest and the days are longer.	In Autumn or Fall the days get colder and shorter. Some plants begin to die and some lose their leaves. Animals move around less. 
Winter is the coldest and the days are shorter. Some plants die and animals hibernate or move to hotter countries. 	In Spring it gets warmer and days get longer. Plants begin to grow and animals start to come back or wake up. 

Talk to your partner about the weather in these pictures.

What is the same and what is different in each season?

■ For more activities, go to Workbook 1 page 92.

Not all countries have four clear seasons. Some have wet and dry seasons. Others seem to have winter or summer all year.

What are the seasons in these photographs? Talk about why you think it is that season.

Which seasons do you have in your country?

Which season is it?

1 Survey the area around your school.

2 Study the plants. Are they starting to grow? Are any losing their leaves?

3 Study the animals. Are there many? Can you see young animals or eggs?

4 Draw what your area looks like now.

5 Predict what it will look like in 6 months. Draw your prediction.

Key idea

The weather and length of day change across the seasons.

■ For more activities, go to Workbook 1 page 93.

Recording rainfall

In this lesson you will explore ways to measure rainfall.

The amount it rains varies around the world. It also varies at different times of the year.

Meteorologists use a rain gauge to record how much rain falls.

A rain gauge

Place	Amount of rainfall in a year (in millimetres)
Dubai, UAE	150
Auckland, New Zealand	1100
Atacama desert, Peru	15
Mawsynram, India	11 800

Look at the table. With a partner, talk about which is the wettest place and which is the driest place.

How will this affect the plants and animals in the area?

■ For more activities, go to Workbook 1 page 94.

Making and testing a rain gauge

1 Make a rain gauge by using the top of a plastic bottle.

2 Add some pebbles to the bottle and add water until they are covered.

3 Turn the top of the bottle over to be a funnel.

4 Tape a ruler to the side of the bottle. Make sure the 0 of the ruler is level with the top of the water you added.

5 Place your rain gauge outside. Choose a place that is open to the sky but not too windy.

6 Check your rain gauge every day.

7 Write down the rainfall in a table like this one.

Day	Amount of rainfall (in millimetres)

8 Talk about any patterns you see in your results.

Be a scientist

Scientists take readings regularly. This is so that no water evaporates from the gauge and changes the results. This helps to make their results fair.

▶ page 8

Key idea

Special instruments can be used to measure the weather.

■ For more activities, go to Workbook 1 page 95.

Observing and measuring the wind

In this lesson you will explore ways to measure the wind and look for patterns.

Key words
anemometer
wind vane

Scientists use equipment to measure the weather.

Making and testing a wind vane

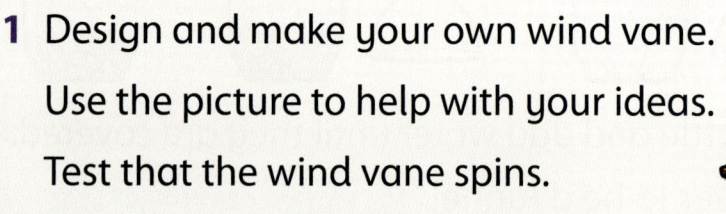

1 Design and make your own wind vane.

   Use the picture to help with your ideas.

   Test that the wind vane spins.

2 Place your wind vane outside.

   Make sure it is not too near trees or buildings.

   Use a compass to find north, south, east and west.

3 Observe the wind direction every day for five days.

   Write down your observations in a table.

Did the wind always blow from the same direction?

Stretch zone

Compare your wind directions with some reported in weather forecasts for your local area.

How could you make your wind vane better?

Be a scientist

Scientists think about how well an investigation has worked. They also suggest improvements.

▶ page 11

■ For more activities, go to Workbook 1 page 96.

Making and testing an anemometer

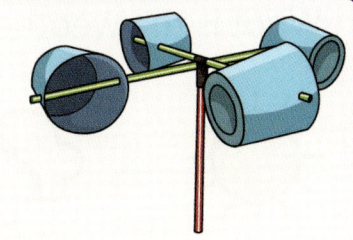

An anemometer tells you how strong the wind is blowing. This is the wind speed.

The cups of the anemometer spin around fast in a strong wind.

1 Design and make an anemometer.

   Test that your anemometer spins.

   You can blow on it or use a hair drier to test it.

2 Take your anemometer outside and measure the speed of the wind.

   Count how many times it spins in 10 seconds.

3 Measure the wind every day for five days.

   Write down your results in a table.

Talk about any patterns in your results. Was every day windy?

Stretch zone

Why is it important to be able to predict the weather?

Key idea

By measuring weather over time we can look for patterns and predict what it is going to be like in the future.

Check how much you know.
Try the puzzles on pages 98–99.

Science fact

The strongest winds on Earth have been measured at over 370 kilometres per hour.

■ For more activities, go to Workbook 1 page 97.

What have I learned about plants and the seasons?

1 What is the weather symbol for rain? Tick the correct answer.

2 Circle the words for the four parts of a plant. Then draw a line from each word to the correct part of the plant.

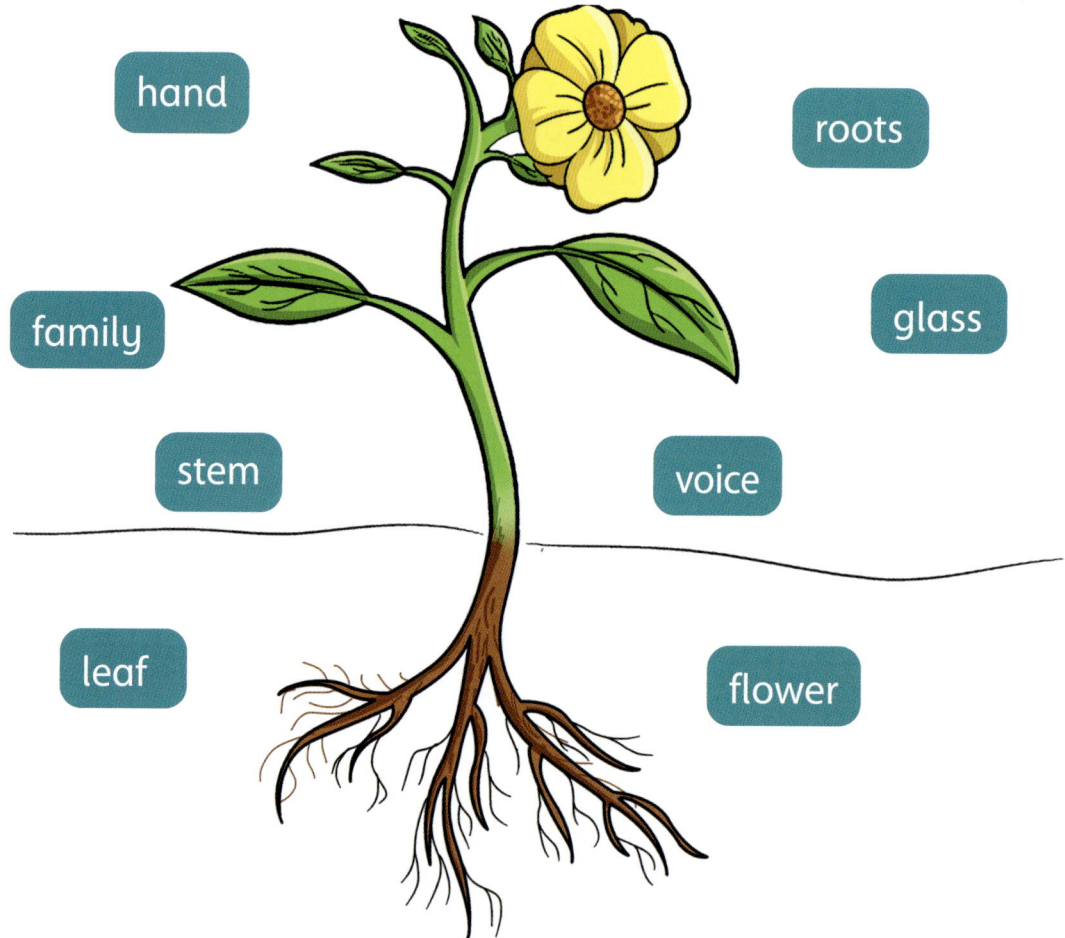

hand

roots

family

glass

stem

voice

leaf

flower

3 Underline the correct answers.

When we eat lettuce we are eating the   flowers / leaves.

Tree stems are called   trunks / roots.

Shrubs are smaller than   flowers / trees.

■ For more activities, go to Workbook 1 page 98.

4 a Which device is used to measure the speed of the wind? Circle the correct picture.

b What is the device called? Complete the word.

a n _ _ o m _ _ _ r

5

a Tick the part of the photograph that shows summer.

b Underline the correct answer.

The day length in summer is usually   short / long.

6 Which person needs to know the weather forecast to do their job?

_____

■ For more activities, go to Workbook 1 page 99.

Glossary

amphibian

animal

bird

body

carnivore

day

deciduous

evergreen

fabric

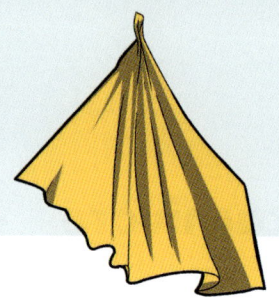

fast

fish

flower

glass

herbivore

human

invertebrate

leaf

loud

mammal

material

metal

move

omnivore

paper

plant

plastic

pull

push

quiet

reptile

rock

roots

season

senses

slow

sound

stem

stop

trunk

vertebrate

voice

water

weather

wild

wood